# C++

# C++

**Anju Bhati**

**CENTRUM PRESS**
NEW DELHI-110002 (INDIA)

**CENTRUM PRESS**
**H.O.:** 4360/4, Ansari Road, Daryaganj,
New Delhi-110002 (India)
Tel: 23278000, 23261597, 23255577, 23286875
**B.O.:** No. 1015, Ist Main Road, BSK IIIrd Stage,
IIIrd Phase, IIIrd Block, Bangalore-560085 (INDIA)
Tel: 080-41723429
*Email:* centrumpress@gmail.com
*Visit us at:* www.centrumpress.com

*C++*



First Edition, 2011

PRINTED IN INDIA

---

*Printed at* Tarun Offset Printers, Delhi-110053

# Contents

# Preface

During the 60s, while computers were still in an early stage of development, many new programming languages appeared. Among them, ALGOL 60, was developed as an alternative to FORTRAN but taking from it some concepts of structured programming which would later inspire most procedural languages, such as CPL and its succesors (like C++). ALGOL 68 also directly influenced the development of data types in C. Nevertheless ALGOL was an non-specific language and its abstraction made it impractical to solve most commercial tasks. In 1963 the CPL (Combined Programming language) appeared with the idea of being more specific for concrete programming tasks of that time than ALGOL or FORTRAN. Nevertheless this same specificity made it a big language and, therefore, difficult to learn and implement.

During the 80s, the C++ language was being refined until it became a language with its own personality. All that with very few losses of compatibility with the code with C, and without resigning to its most important characteristics. In fact, the ANSI standard for the C language published in 1989 took good part of the contributions of C++ to structured programming. C++ has been evolving, and a new version of the standard, c++0x, is being developed to be published soon, with several new features.

*Author*

# Preface

# 1

# Programming Language

## ABC LANGUAGE

The Fortran, as the name suggests, is best suited for numerical computations. That is why it is popular among physicists, chemists, mathematicians and engineers. The handling of alphanumeric strings is not so good in fortran but that is not such a handicap because one doesn't need this aspect very much while doing numerical computations. Like any language FORTRAN has its syntax and that is what we shall be learning here. We shall be following a utilitarian approach so we shall not dwell much on the structure of fortran per se but we shall learn fortran by using it.

So, in the following, shall introduce some concepts and immediately give examples to illustrate the concept. The way the fortran programmes are used on computers is as follows. First one makes (writes) a fortran programme on computer. That is, one creates a file containing a collection of fortran statements. Invariably a fortran programme has.f or.f77 as an ending character string (extension). The computer cannot understand this fortran programme as such and it has to be converted into a programme that the computer understands. This is done by a fortran compiler and the process is called compilation of the programme.

The translated programme is in machine language and often called as a.out. But it can have any name. Before the compiler creates a machine language programme, it creates an intermediate file which has an ending.o. This file is called the object code. So, let us assume that you have made a programme called*foo.f* (Here foo is a generic name of a file. That is, foo can be replaced by any character string). On compilation, an object file *foo.o* and an executable a.out is created by the computer. Other possible names of the compiler are fort, g77, f90, lf90 (only in the Institute of Physics and on some of the machines) etc. The output of the command is foo.o and a.out. To run the programme, type,

a.out

or

./a.out

at the command prompt. The programme will then be executed.

*The steps involved in computing using fortran*:

- Make a programme file (eg *foo.f* ) using any editor of your choice
- Compile the file and make an object code ( *foo.o* ) and an executable file
  (usually *a.out* )
- Execute the programme ( *a.out* )
- Check the results for errors, correct the errors in the fortran programme and go back to step 2

The Fortran compiler, by default, creates executable file named a.out after compilation. The problem with default is every compiled file is a.out so one doesn't know what it does if you have a number of programmes.

Also, every time you compile a new programme, old a.out is erased and new a.out is written in it's place. So, it is convinient to follow a convention where the executable of a Fortran programme has a name similar to the name of the fortran programme. The convention I follow is to name the executable as foo.

*The command to generate this executable is:*

f77 –o foo foo.f

It appears that the object file foo.o is of no use. As mentioned above, the object file is a programme which is between a fortran programme and its executable code. It is useful when one has a number of subunits (subroutines, functions, libraries) in a fortran programme and if one is modifying only a part of a programme, it doesn't make sense to compile all the other programme units again and again. In this case, one can compile the programme that is changed and use link the object code thus created with the object codes of other programme units.

This saves a lot of compilation time, particularly if one has tens of other programme units. During the course of these lectures we will not be dealing with complicated and lengthy programmes and as a result we will not be using the object files in the course. The C++ manual has introduced the C++ library. When using this library to solve a particular system it is necessary to write the C++ code that allows to deal with the system at hand.

The primary purpose of the Maple library was to allow the automatic generation of the C++ code being given the Maple description of an equations system and then to compile and run the generated code in order to get the result within the Maple session. But when developing this library it appears that the use of symbolic computation may allow to increase the efficiency of the C++ solving procedure. Hence the procedures available in the Maple library may be divided into two categories:

- Procedures that allow to solve a given problem. In that case the procedure will:
  - Generate the necessary C++ code
  - Compile this code
  - Run the created programme
  - Return the result to Maple
- Procedures that allow to improve the efficiency of a solving procedure (which may eventually use C++ programme).

The Maple library ALIAS.m has initially been developed by Didier Bondyfalat. ALIAS-Maple is compiled for Maple V.5 and 9.5 and this version has 49356 lines of code. In this package there are numerous Maple procedures that may be used to solve or to help to solve a specific problem. The behaviour of these procedures may be modified by changing the values of some Maple variables (that will correspond to the parameters of the ALIAS-C++ procedures). An ALIAS-Maple variable is always defined using the following syntax:

'ALIAS/XX'

The use of some of these variables may need an understanding of the algorithms of ALIAS-C++.

The C++ procedures created by ALIAS-Maple procedures have usually a fixed name (e.g. _GS_ for the general purpose solving procedures) but this behaviour may be changed for some of them if the string variable 'ALIAS/ID' is defined (and on the long term it is planned that all ALIAS-Maple procedures will propose this possibility): in that case all files created by a procedure have the 'ALIAS/ID' string appended to their name.

*Before explaining how to use this package very important remarks have to be done*:

- An equation f(x) = 0 is defined in ALIAS-Maple by f(x) while an inequality is defined by $f(x) \leq 0$
- Not all expression may interval evaluated. For example interval evaluating 1/x with x being an interval including 0 will cause the C++ programme created by ALIAS-Maple to crash. ALIAS-Maple provides procedures to deal with this problem.
- It has been noticed that for large expressions the compilation time of their C++ equivalent may be quite large (or even may be impossible). It is sometime possible to avoid this problem by turning off the optimization flag. Indeed by default the C++ programme will be compiled with the optimization flag -O and it is sometime better to turn off this option by setting the flag 'ALIAS/optimized' to 0. Another approach is to use some procedures provided in ALIAS-Maple that simplify the compilation by using dummy intervals or decompose expression into elementary components as will be seen later on. This problem may also be solved by using the ALIAS parser in order to avoid having to compile very large expressions.

The reader interested only in the solving procedures available in ALIAS-Maple may skip to chapter. But the concept of simplification procedures explained are worth considering afterward as they may drastically improve the efficiency of the algorithms. This manual describes the use of the ALIAS Maple library both for version 5.5 and for version 9.5, with minor difference when loading the library. This interface is intended to be used through a command line and not a worksheet.

## OBJECT-ORIENTED PROGRAMMING

Object oriented programming is different from from procedural programming languages like C, Pascal in several ways. Everything in OOPs is grouped as "Objects". OOP's, defined in the purest sence, is implemented by sending messages to Objects

*The different set of components or characteristics of OOP as follows*:

- Object Entity
- Abstraction
- Encapsulation
- Inheritance
- Polymorphism

### OBJECT ENTITY

An Object is an instance of a class or it can be considered a "thing that can perform a set of activities". In this world everything is Object. Object is an identifiable entity which has some characterstics as well as behaviour. For example a car is an object which has characteristics like its shape, colour, weight, size, model and behaviour i.e. moveability of car.

The object's interface consists of a set of commands, each command performing a specific action. An object asks another object to perform an action by sending it a message. The requesting(sending) object is refered as *sender* and the receiving object is refered as *receiver*.

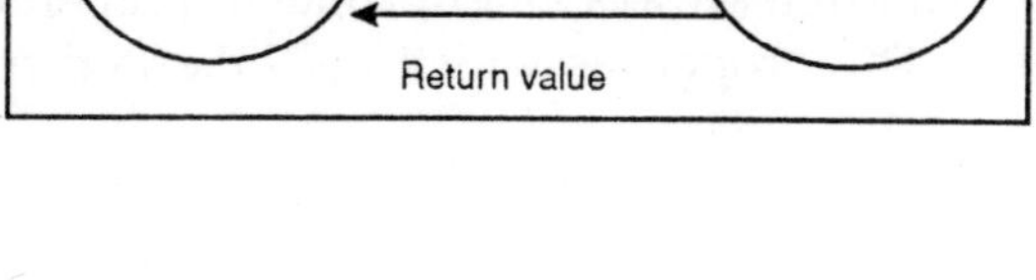

In the above diagram the control is passed to the receiving object until it completes the command; control then returns to the sending object.

## ABSTRACTION

Abstraction is an act to representing the essential features of an object without including the internal details or explanations. It is the most powerfull paradism of OOP's. In other words Abstarction means hiding something but exist in reality.

For example there is a switch board having various switches and ask to student to switch on the fan. When the student press the switch of fan, he does not knows what is hapening inside the switchboard. He just knows about the essential features to switch on the fan. What is hapening inside that is abstraction.

The Abstraction is used in C++ by concept. The Class is the combination of data members and member functions.

The characteristics of an Object is represented in Class as its variables which we can define under the section *i.e.* Private, Public and Protected and behaviour is represented in class as member function.

## ENCAPSULATION

The encapsulation can be implemented in C++ by using Class concept. As we knows a Class is the combination of data member and member functions, the member functions always operate on the data members which is to be declared in the same class as a single unit is called Encapsulation. In other words Encapsulation means wrapping up of data members and member functions into a single unit.

## INHERITANCE

The idea of Inheritance derived from the concept of Classes. It is the process by which the object of one class acquire the property of object of an another class.

Like the children always inherit some of properties from their parents. The properties which are inherited from the parent class is called Base class and the child class which acquires these properties is called derived class.

*There are five types of Inheritance*:

1. Single Inheritance
2. Multilevel Inheritance
3. Multiple Inheritance
4. Hierarchical Inheritance
5. Hybrid Inheritance

## POLYMORPHISM

Polymorphism is an another important concept of OOP's. The word *Poly* originated from Greek word many and *morphism* from the Greek word forms and thus polymorphism means many forms. Polymorphism allows many different types of Objects to perform the same operation by responding to the same message.

It is the process of defining number of objects of different classes into a group and call the methods to carry out the operation of the objects using different function calls. This concept is implemented in C++ by using Function Overloadind, Operator Overloading, Virtual Functions etc.

## EXAMPLE

Let's say if the programme has a card deck for a simple blackjack game we are programming. Remember*containership* and *inheritance*? Let's think about the types of parts that make up a deck and those are the cards. Since all of the cards are very similar in structure, we could use a struct to represent a single card:

```
enum Suit = {Clubs, Spades, Diamonds, Hearts};
struct Card
{
   Suit suit;
   char digit;
};
```

A note on the digit. If digit <= 10, then it is a number, else it is the letter of the card (J, Q, K, A). You could also use it as a number 1(ace) through 13(king) as well, perhaps if you were using the card value in additions or such. A simple object, the card deck only has one type of item. Now let's think about the types of actions you can perform on the deck, and then make a class declaration out of this list, as well as using the previously declared data.

```
class Deck
{
public:
   void CreateDeck(); . // Fills array with
   legal cards
   void Shuffle();   // Shuffles those cards
   Card DrawCard();  // Gets a card from the
   deck
 private:
   Card cards[52];
};
```

Now we have considered all of the things we may need to use a card deck. The programmer first sets up the deck with CreateDeck(), then whenever needed can Shuffle() the deck, and when the dealer deals a card, it can be picked up using DrawCard(), and then perhaps placed in the players hand (which could also could be a class too) or whatever the programmer needs to do with it.

A constructor is declared by creating a function by the same name as the class. The destructor has the same name, except with a ~ (the tlide key, next to the 1) in front of it. Below is the modified Deck class which takes advantage of C++ constructors and destructors.

The array change to a pointer is to allow for dynamic memory allocation using the new command, to show a very common use of the constructor and destructor:

```
class Deck
{
public:
        Deck();         // Constructor
        ~Deck();        // Destructor
   void CreateDeck(); . // Fills array with
   legal cards
```

```
    void Shuffle();   // Shuffles those cards
    Card DrawCard();  // Gets a card from the
    deck
  private:
    Card* cards;
  };
```

Notice that obviously the constructor does not return anything, since it is an "invisible function" which is automatically called when you make the statement Deck MyCardDeck;. The same is true for the destructor, which is called when the variable goes out of scope. Below is an example of how to define and code a constructor, where the array is allocated and the data is initalized, and the destructor compliment, which cleans up what the constructor did:

```
Deck::Deck()
{
  cards = new Card[52]; // Allocate memory
  CreateDeck();         // Set up the deck
}
Deck::~Deck()
{
  delete[] cards;       //   Deallocate
  memory
}
```

Notice that all methods and members of the class are available in the constructor and destructor, just as in every other function. Intclass.cc, executable in any DOS compiler or console mode win32 compiler shows exactly when these functions are called, and also shows many other concepts which will be explained later in this tutorial.

Let's return to our earler counter example which did not have a constructor but which really needed one, or at least a SetCounter() function. We can create a constructor to start the counter at zero, as well as starting it off at a value the user can enter:

```
class Counter
{
public:
```

```
            Counter();        //basic constructor
            Counter(int x);//set the counter
            SetCount(int x);. //sets the count
        void Count() {CurrentCount++;}
        int ReadDisplay() {return CurrentCount;}
    private:
        int CurrentCount;
    };
```

Some of you who don't know about *overloaded* functions may think two Counter() functions is an error, but it's not! In C++, two functions with the same name can be declared (this applies everywhere, not just classes), as long as the compiler can descern between which function is being called.

In the case of the constructor, you must use this feature since the constructor must be the same name as the class. Also note that a destructor was not declared since there is nothing we need to clean up — the compiler already has a default destructor for the int data type (CurrentCount). Let's see how we should write the code for these functions:

```
Counter::Counter()
{
    SetCount(0);
}
Counter::Counter(int x)
{
    SetCount(x);
}
Counter::SetCount(int x)
{
    CurrentCount = x;
}
```

After seeing it in code, things become a little clearer. You can overload as many times as you want to pass different things into the constructor, just be sure that they have a different number of parameters. It is technically possible to have them with the same number, but since some basic data types can change into others (like int to float or similar), the function call becomes *ambigous*, and the compiler doesn't know which to use and generates an error – so it's best just to steer clear of overloaded functions of the same number of parameters.

You may wonder why it went through the trouble of calling SetCount() from the constructor functions, and the reason is data hiding. You may understand now why to hide data from the outside – but now the inside? It may seem a little riduclous but imagine our card deck example, when I mentioned two possible formats in the deck.

Well what if I decided, because of some reason that I wanted to store the text representation of the counter, for easy display on a webpage or something similar, rather than in a native computer form. If I had used CurrentCount in all three of the above functions, I would have to rewrite three functions to compensate for the change. But instead I used SetCount(), so I would now only have to rewrite one.

Of course this is a small example and that wouldn't be much hassle, but imagine if I had a medium sized to large class of 20 or more functions and 5 or so variables, and I used the most direct route.

That's a lot to change, and I myself have encountered times where I had classes this large or larger in the Project V2143 game where I wanted to change the way the data was stored, say in the terrain, or in the save game file, I would have to rewrite all my functions again.

Then I started calling functions like I did above and then when I changed formats, all I had to do was change 5 or so lines out of my tens of thousands to make a major change to the game, and that was a good feeling not having to recode all of my stuff again.

So even though it looks a little silly and out-of-the-way, doing it the above way will end up saving you a lot of time in the long run, as I had to learn the hard way myself. This is the main downfall of OOP, calling the functions and going the longer route through one set of code instead of reworking the same set over and set is slower because you can't optimize as much, as well as the overhead of calling the functions. But it's worth saving a few hours of programming time for that extra.05 or.1fps gain you get in the end — and me, being the speed freak I am, had to accept that. You would be surprised how much speed you could pull out of the computer if you spent the time optimizing — but at some point your effort doesn't make up for the extra execution speed, and that's your decision to make.

## VARIABLES

A variable is a symbolic name for a memory location in which data can be stored and subsequently recalled. Variables are used for holding data values so that they can be utilized in various computations in a programme. The value of variable can change during the exectution of programme.

*All variables have two important attributes*:

- A type which is established when the variable is defined (*e.g.*, integer, real, character). Once defined, the type of a C++ variable cannot be changed.
- A value which can be changed by assigning a new value to the variable. The kind of values a variable can assume depends on its type. For example, an integer variable can only take integer values (*e.g.*, 2, 100, -12). Listing 1.2 illustrates the uses of some simple variable.

**Listing 1.2**

```
# include <iostream.h>
int main (void)
{
        int workDays;
        float workHours, payRate, weeklyPay;
        workDays = 5;
        workHours = 7.5;
        payRate = 38.55;
        weeklyPay = workDays * workHours *
payRate;
        cout << "Weekly Pay = ";
        cout << weeklyPay;
        cout << '\n';
}
```

## Annotation

4. This line defines an int (integer) variable called workDays, which will represent the number of working days in a week. As a general rule, a variable is defined by specifying its type first, followed by the variable name, followed by a semicolon.
5. This line defines three float (real) variables which, respectively, represent the work hours per day, the hourly pay rate, and the weekly pay. As illustrated by this line, multiple variables of the same type can be defined at once by separating them with commas.
6. This line is an assignment statement. It assigns the value 5 to the variable workDays. Therefore, after this statement is executed, workDays denotes the value 5.
7. This line assigns the value 7.5 to the variable workHours.
8. This line assigns the value 38.55 to the variable payRate.
9. This line calculates the weekly pay as the product of workDays, workHours, and payRate (* is the multiplication operator). The resulting value is stored in weeklyPay.

10-12. These lines output three items in sequence: the string "Weekly Pay = ", the value of the variable weeklyPay, and a newline character. When run, the programme will produce the following output:

```
Weekly Pay = 1445.625
```

When a variable is defined, its value is undefined until it is actually assigned one. For example, weeklyPay has an undefined value/unpredictable value (*i.e.*, whatever happens to be in the memory location which the variable denotes at the time) until line 9 is executed. The assigning of a value to a variable for the first time is called.

## INITIALIZATION

It is important to ensure that a variable is initialized before it is used in any computation. It is possible to define a variable and initialize it at the same time. This is considered a good programming practice, because it pre-empts the possibility of using the variable prior to it being initialized.

Listing 1.3 is a revised version of Listing 1.2 which uses this technique. For all intents and purposes, the two programmes are equivalent.

**Listing 1.3**

```
#include <iostream.h>
int main (void)
{
    int workDays = 5;
    float workHours = 7.5;
    float payRate = 38.55;
    float weeklyPay = workDays * workHours *
          payRate;
    cout << "Weekly Pay = ";
    cout << weeklyPay;
    cout << '\n';
}
```

## SIMPLE INPUT/OUTPUT

The most common way in which a programme communicates with the outside world is through simple, character-oriented Input/Output (IO) operations.

C++ provides two useful operators for this purpose: >> for input and << for output. We have already seen examples of output using <<. Listing 1.4 also illustrates the use of >> for input.

**Listing 1.4**

```
#include <iostream.h>
int main (void)
{
    int workDays = 5;
    float workHours = 7.5;
    float payRate, weeklyPay;
    cout << "What is the hourly pay rate? ";
    cin >> payRate;
```

```
9     weeklyPay = workDays * workHours *
      payRate;
10    cout << "Weekly Pay = ";
11    cout << weeklyPay;
12    cout << '\n';
13 }
```

## Annotation

7. This line outputs the prompt What is the hourly pay rate? to seek user input.
8. This line reads the input value typed by the user and copies it to payRate. The input operator >> takes an input stream as its left operand (cin is the standard C++ input stream which corresponds to data entered via the keyboard) and a variable (to which the input data is copied) as its right operand.

9-13. The rest of the programme is as before. When run, the programme will produce the following output (user input appears in bold):

```
What is the hourly pay rate? 33.55
Weekly Pay = 1258.125
```

Both << and >> return their left operand as their result, enabling multiple input or multiple output operations to be combined into one statement. This is illustrated by Listing 1.5 which now allows the input of both the daily work hours and the hourly pay rate.

## Listing 1.5

```
#include <iostream.h>
int main (void)
{
   int workDays = 5;
   float workHours, payRate, weeklyPay;
   cout << "What are the work hours and the
         hourly pay rate? ";
   cin >> workHours >> payRate;
   weeklyPay = workDays * workHours *
   payRate;
```

```
9     cout << "Weekly Pay = " << weeklyPay <<
      '\n';
10 }
```

**Annotation**

7 This line reads two input values typed by the user and copies them to workHours and payRate, respectively. The two values should be separated by white space (*i.e.*, one or more space or tab characters). This statement is equivalent to:

```
(cin >> workHours) >> payRate;
```

Because the result of >> is its left operand, (cin >> workHours) evaluates to cin which is then used as the left operand of the next >> operator.

9 This line is the result of combining lines 10-12 from Listing 1.4. It outputs "Weekly Pay = ", followed by the value of weeklyPay, followed by a newline character. This statement is equivalent to:

```
((cout << "Weekly Pay = ") << weeklyPay) <<
      '\n';
```

Because the result of << is its left operand, (cout << "Weekly Pay = ") evaluates to cout which is then used as the left operand of the next << operator, etc.

When run, the programme will produce the following output:

```
What are the work hours and the hourly pay
   rate? 7.5 33.55
Weekly Pay = 1258.125.
```

## COMMENTS

A comment is a piece of descriptive text which explains some aspect of a programme. Programme comments are totally ignored by the compiler and are only intended for human readers.

C++ *provides two types of comment delimiters*:

- Anything after//(until the end of the line on which it appears) is considered a comment.
- Anything enclosed by the pair/* and */is considered a comment.

## Listing 1.6

```
#include <iostream.h>
/* This programme calculates the weekly gross pay for a worker,
   based on the total number of hours worked and the hourly pay
   rate. */
int main (void)
{
   int   workDays = 5;     // Number of work days per week
   float workHours = 7.5;        // Number of work hours per day
   float payRate = 33.50;        // Hourly pay rate
   float weeklyPay;        // Gross weekly pay
   weeklyPay = workDays * workHours * payRate;
   cout << "Weekly Pay = " << weeklyPay << '\n';
}
```

Comments should be used to enhance (not to hinder) the readability of a programme.

*The following two points, in particular, should be noted*:

- A comment should be easier to read and understand than the code which it tries to explain. A confusing or unnecessarily-complex comment is worse than no comment at all.
- Over-use of comments can lead to even less readability. A programme which contains so much comment that you can hardly see the code can by no means be considered readable.
- Use of descriptive names for variables and other entities in a programme, and proper indentation of the code can reduce the need for using comments. The

best guideline for how to use comments is to simply apply common sense.

## MEMORY

A computer provides a Random Access Memory (RAM) for storing executable programme code as well as the data that programme manipulates. This memory can be thought of as a contiguous sequence of bits, each of which is capable of storing a binary digit (0 or 1). Typically, the memory is also divided into groups of 8 consecutive bits (called bytes). The bytes are sequentially addressed. Therefore each byte can be uniquely identified by its address

The C++ compiler generates executable code which maps data entities to memory locations. For example, the variable definition int salary = 65000; causes the compiler to allocate a few bytes to represent salary. The exact number of bytes allocated and the method used for the binary representation of the integer depends on the specific C++ implementation, but let us say two bytes encoded as a 2's complement integer. The compiler uses the *address* of the first byte at which salary is allocated to refer to it. The above assignment causes the value 65000 to be stored as a 2's complement integer in the two bytes allocated.

While the exact binary representation of a data item is rarely of interest to a programmer, the general organization of memory and use of addresses for referring to data items (as we will see later) is very important.

## INTEGER DATA TYPE

An integer variable may be defined to be of type short, int, or long. The only difference is that an int uses more or at least the same number of bytes as a short, and a long uses more or at least the same number of bytes as an int. For example, on the author's PC, a short uses 2 bytes, an int also 2 bytes, and a long 4 bytes.

```
short    age = 20;
int      salary = 65000;
long     price = 4500000;
```

By default, an integer variable is assumed to be signed (*i.e.*, have a signed representation so that it can assume positive as well as negative values).

However, an integer can be defined to be unsigned by using the keyword unsigned in its definition. The keyword signed is also allowed but is redundant.

```
unsigned shortage = 20;
unsigned int  salary = 65000;
unsigned long price = 4500000;
```

A literal integer (*e.g.*, 1984) is always assumed to be of type int, unless it has an L or l suffix, in which case it is treated as a long. Also, a literal integer can be specified to be unsigned using the suffix U or u.

*For example*:

```
1984L    1984l    1984U    1984u    1984LU
   1984ul
```

Literal integers can be expressed as follows:

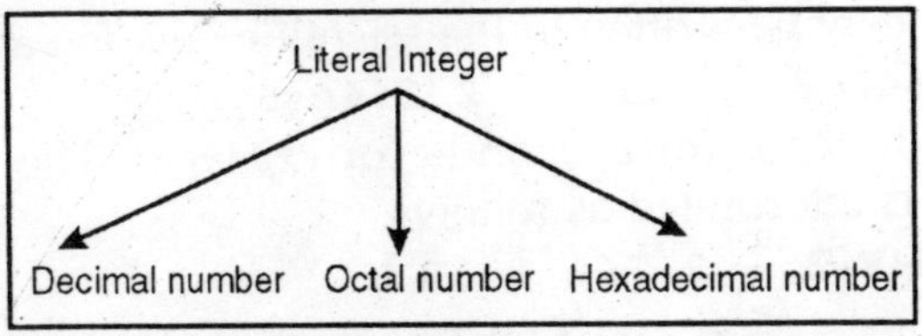


The decimal number is the one we have been using so far. An integer is taken to be octal if it is preceded by a zero (0), and hexadecimal if it is preceded by a 0x or 0X. For example:

```
92      // decimal
0134    // equivalent octal
0x5C    // equivalent hexadecimal
```

Octal numbers use the base 8, and can therefore only use the digits 0-7.

Hexadecimal numbers use the base 16, and therefore use the digit 0-9 and letter A-F (or a-f) to represent, respectively, 10-15. Octal and hexadecimal numbers are calculated as follows:

$$0134 = 1 \times 8^2 + 3 \times 8^1 + 4 \times 8^0 = 64 + 24 + 4 = 92$$

$$0x5C = 5 \times 16^1 + 12 \times 16^0 = 80 + 12 = 92$$

## FLOAT DATA TYPE

A real variable may be defined to be of type float or double. The latter uses more bytes and therefore offers a greater range and accuracy for representing real numbers. For example, on the author's PC, a float uses 4 and a double uses 8 bytes.

```
float    interestRate = 0.06;
double   pi = 3.141592654;
```

A literal real (*e.g.*, 0.06) is always assumed to be of type double, unless it has an F or f suffix, in which case it is treated as a float, or an L or l suffix, in which case it is treated as a long double. The latter uses more bytes than a double for better accuracy (*e.g.*, 10 bytes on the author's PC). For example:

```
0.06F      0.06f      3.141592654L
   3.141592654l
```

In addition to the decimal notation used so far, literal reals may also be expressed in *scientific* notation. For example, 0.002164 may be written in the scientific notation as:

```
2.164E-3     or     2.164e-3
```

The letter E (or e) stands for *exponent*. The scientific notation is interpreted as follows:

```
2.164E-3 = 2.164 × 10⁻³
```

## CHARACTERS

A character variable is defined to be of type char. A character variable occupies a single byte which contains the *code* for the character. This code is a numeric value and depends on the *character coding system* being used (*i.e.*, is machine-dependent). The most common system is ASCII (American Standard Code for Information Interchange). For example, the character *A* has the ASCII code 65, and the character *a* has the ASCII code 97.

```
char     ch = 'A';
```

Like integers, a character variable may be specified to be signed or unsigned. By default (on most systems) char means signed char. However, on some systems it may mean unsigned char. A signed character variable can hold numeric values in the range -128 through 127. An unsigned character variable can hold numeric values in the range 0 through 255. As a result, both are often used to represent small integers in programmes (and can be assigned numeric values like integers):

```
signed char   offset = -88;
unsigned char row = 2, column = 26;
```

A literal character is written by enclosing the character between a pair of single quotes (*e.g.*, 'A'). Nonprintable characters are represented using escape sequences. For example:

```
'\n'  // new line
'\r'  // carriage return
'\t'  // horizontal tab
'\v'  // vertical tab
'\b'  // backspace
'\f'  // formfeed
```

Single and double quotes and the backslash character can also use the escape notation:

```
'\''  //single quote (')
'\"'  //double quote (")
'\\'  //backslash (\)
```

Literal characters may also be specified using their numeric code value. The general escape sequence \ooo (*i.e.*, a backslash followed by up to three octal digits) is used for this purpose. For example (assuming ASCII):

```
'\12'   //newline (decimal code = 10)
'\11'   //horizontal tab (decimal code = 9)
'\101'  //'A' (decimal code = 65)
'\0'    //null (decimal code = 0)
```

## STRINGS

A string is a consecutive sequence (*i.e., array*) of characters which are terminated by a null character. A string variable is defined to be of type char* (*i.e.*, a *pointer* to character). A pointer is simply the address of a memory location. (Pointers will be discussed in Chapter 5). A string variable, therefore, simply contains the address of where the first character of a string appears.

*For example, consider the definition*:

```
char    *str = "HELLO";
```

A literal string is written by enclosing its characters between a pair of double quotes (*e.g.*, "HELLO"). The compiler always appends a null character to a literal string to mark its end. The characters of a string may be specified using any of the notations for specifying literal characters.

*For example*:

```
"Name\tAddress\tTelephone"                    / /
   tab-separated words
"ASCII character 65: \101"                   // 'A'
   specified as '101'
```

A long string may extend beyond a single line, in which case each of the preceding lines should be terminated by a backslash. For example:

```
"Example to show \
the use of backslash for \
writing a long string"
```

The backslash in this context means that the rest of the string is continued on the next line. The above string is equivalent to the single line string:

```
"Example to show the use of backslash for
   writing a long string"
```

A common programming error results from confusing a single-character string (*e.g.*, "A") with a single character (*e.g.*, 'A'). These two are *not* equivalent. The former consists of two bytes (the character 'A' followed by the character '\0'), whereas the latter consists of a single byte. The shortest possible string is the null string ("") which simply consists of the null character.

## NAMES

Programming languages use names to refer to the various entities that make up a programme. We have already seen examples of an important category of such names (*i.e.*, variable names). Other categories include: function names, type names, and macro names, which will be described later in this book.

Names are a programming convenience, which allow the programmer to organize what would otherwise be quantities of plain data into a meaningful and human-readable collection.

As a result, no trace of a name is left in the final executable code generated by a compiler. For example, a temperature variable eventually becomes a few bytes of memory which is referred to by the executable code by its address, not its name.

C++ imposes the following rules for creating valid names (also called identifiers). A name should consist of one or more characters, each of which may be a letter (*i.e.*, 'A'-'Z' and 'a'-'z'), a digit (*i.e.*, '0'-'9'), or an underscore character ('_'), except that the first character may not be a digit. Upper and lower case letters are distinct.

*For example*: Salary//valid identifier

```
salary2  // valid identifier
2salary  // invalid identifier  (begins with
   a digit)
_salary  // valid identifier
Salary   // valid but distinct  from salary
```

C++ imposes no limit on the number of characters in an identifier. However, most implementation do. But the limit is usually so large that it should not cause a concern (*e.g.*, 255 characters).

Certain words are reserved by C++ for specific purposes and may not be used as identifiers. These are called reserved words or keywords:

| | | | | | |
|---|---|---|---|---|---|
| asm | continue | float | new | signed | try |
| auto | default | for | operator | sizeof | typedef |
| break | delete | friend | private | static | union |
| case | do | goto | protected | struct | unsigned |
| catch | double | if | public | switch | virtual |
| char | else | inline | register | template | void |
| class | enum | int | return | this | volatile |
| const | extern | long | short | throw | while |

## QUESTIONS

Q1. Write a programme which inputs a temperature reading expressed in Fahrenheit and outputs its equivalent in Celsius, using the formula:

$$°C = \frac{5}{9}(°F - 32)$$

Compile and run the programme. Its behaviour should resemble this:

```
Temperature in Fahrenheit:                41
degrees Fahrenheit = 5 degrees Celsius
```

Q2. Which of the following represent valid variable definitions?

```
int n = -100;
unsigned int i = -100;
signed int = 2.9;
long m = 2, p = 4;
int 2k;
double x = 2 * m;
float y = y * 2;
unsigned double z = 0.0;
double d = 0.67F;
float f = 0.52L;
signed char = -1786;
char c = '$' + 2;
sign char h = '\111';
char *name = "Peter Pan";
unsigned char *num = "276811";
```

Q3. Which of the following represent valid identifiers?

```
identifier
seven_11
_unique_
gross-income
gross$income
2by2
default
average_weight_of_a_large_pizza
variable
object.oriented
```

Q4. Define variables to represent the following entities:

- Age of a person.
- Income of an employee.
- Number of words in a dictionary.
- A letter of the alphabet.
- A greeting message.

## ANSWERS

1.
```
#include <iostream.h>
int main (void)
{
     double fahrenheit;
     double celsius;
     cout << "Temperature in Fahrenhait:
";
     cin >> fahrenheit;
     celsius = 5 * (fahrenheit - 32)/9;
     cout << fahrenheit << " degrees
Fahrenheit = "
          << celsius << " degrees
Celsius\n";
     return 0;
}
```

2.
```
int n = -100;                // valid
unsigned int i = -100;  // valid
signed int = 2.9;                        //
invalid: no variable name
long m = 2, p = 4;          // valid
int 2k;                      // invalid: 2k not
an identifier
double x = 2 * m;                        //
valid
float y = y * 2;                         //
valid (but dangerous!)
unsigned double z = 0.0;                 //
invalid: can't be unsigned
double d = 0.67F;                        //
valid
float f = 0.52L;             // valid
signed char = -1786;    // invalid: no
variable name
char c = '$' + 2;                        //
valid
sign char h = '\111';   // invalid: 'sign'
not recognized
```

```
    char *name = "Peter Pan";// valid
    unsigned char *num = "276811";// valid
3.  identifier                  // valid
    seven_11                    // valid
    _unique_                    // valid
    gross-income                // invalid: - not
    allowed in id
    gross$income                // invalid: $ not
    allowed in id
    2by2                        // invalid: can't
    start with digit
    default                     // invalid: default
    is a keyword
    average_weight_of_a_large_pizza// valid
    variable                    // valid
    object.oriented             // invalid:. not
    allowed in id
4.  int  age;                   //age of a person
    double    employeeIncome;//employee income
    long wordsInDictn;          //number of words
    in dictionary
    char letter;                //letter    of
    alphabet
    char *greeting;             //greeting message
```

# 2

# Expressions and Statements

## OPERATORS

C++ provides operators for composing arithmetic, relational, logical, bitwise, and conditional expressions. It also provides operators which produce useful sideeffects, such as assignment, increment, and decrement. We will look at each category of operators in turn. We will also discuss the precedence rules which govern the order of operator evaluation in a multi-operator expression.

## ARITHMETIC OPERATORS

C++ provides five basic arithmetic operators.

| Operator | Name | Example | |
|---|---|---|---|
| + | Addition | 12 + 4.9 | // gives 16.9 |
| – | Subtraction | 3.98 - 4 | // gives –0.02 |
| * | Multiplication | 2 * 3.4 | // gives 6.8 |
| / | Division | 9/2.0 | // gives 4.5 |
| % | Remainder | 13 % 3 | // gives 1 |

Except for remainder (%) all other arithmetic operators can accept a mix of integer and real operands. Generally, if both operands are integers then the result will be an integer. However, if one or both of the operands are reals then the result will be a real (or double to be exact). When both operands of the division operator (/) are integers then the division is performed as an integer division and not the normal division we are used to. Integer division always results in an integer outcome (*i.e.*, the result is always rounded down).

*For example*:

```
9/2      // gives 4, not 4.5!
-9/2 // gives -5, not -4!
```

Unintended integer divisions are a common source of programming errors. To obtain a real division when both operands are integers, you should cast one of the operands to be real:

```
int      cost = 100;
int      volume = 80;
double   unitPrice = cost / (double) volume;
   // gives 1.25
```

The remainder operator (%) expects integers for both of its operands. It returns the remainder of integer-dividing the operands. For example 13%3 is calculated by integer dividing 13 by 3 to give an outcome of 4 and a remainder of 1; the result is therefore 1.

It is possible for the outcome of an arithmetic operation to be too large for storing in a designated variable. This situation is called an overflow. The outcomeof an overflow is machine-dependent and therefore undefined.

*For example*:

```
unsigned char k = 10 * 92;//overflow: 920 >
   255
```

It is illegal to divide a number by zero. This results in a run-time *division-byzero* failure which typically causes the programme to terminate.

## RELATIONAL OPERATORS

C++ provides six relational operators for comparing numeric quantities. These are summarized in Table 2.3. Relational operators evaluate to 1 (representing the *true* outcome) or 0 (representing the *false* outcome).

**Table Relational Operators.**

| Operator | Name | Example | |
|---|---|---|---|
| == | Equality | 5 == 5 | **//gives 1 t.e. true** |
| != | Inequality | **5 != 5** | **//gives 0 t.e. false** |
| < | Less than | **5 < 5.5** | **//gives 1 t.e. true** |

| | | | |
|---|---|---|---|
| <= | Less than or equal | **5 <= 5** | **//gives 1 t.e. true** |
| > | Greater than | **5 > 5.5** | **//gives 0 t.e. false** |
| >= | Greater than or equal | **6.3 >= 5** | **//gives 1 t.e. true** |

Note that the <= and >= operators are only supported in the form shown. In particular, =< and => are both invalid and do not mean anything. The operands of a relational operator must evaluate to a number. Characters are valid operands since they are represented by numeric values. For example (assuming ASCII coding):

```
'A' < 'F'//gives 1 (is like 65 < 70) t.e.
   true
```

The relational operators should not be used for comparing strings, because this will result in the string *addresses* being compared, not the string contents.

For example, the expression

```
"HELLO" < "BYE"
```

Causes the address of "HELLO" to be compared to the address of "BYE". As these addresses are determined by the compiler (in a machine-dependent manner), the outcome may be 0 or may be 1, and is therefore undefined. C++ provides library functions (*e.g.*, strcmp) for the lexicographic comparison of string. These will be described later in the book.

## LOGICAL OPERATORS

C++ provides three logical operators for combining logical expression. These are summarized in table like the relational operators, logical operators evaluate to 1 or 0.

**Table Logical Operators.**

<table>
<tr><th>Operator</th><th>Name</th><th>Example</th><th></th></tr>
<tr><td>!</td><td>Logical negation</td><td>!(5 == 5)</td><td>//gives 0</td></tr>
<tr><td>&&</td><td>Logical and</td><td>5 < 6 && 6 < 6</td><td>//gives 1</td></tr>
<tr><td>||</td><td>Logical or</td><td>5 < 6 || 6 < 5</td><td>//gives 1</td></tr>
</table>

Logical *negation* is a unary operator, which negates the logical value of its single operand. If its operand is nonzero it produce 0, and if it is 0 it produces 1. Logical *and* produces 0 if one or both of its operands evaluate to 0. Otherwise, it produces 1. Logical *or* produces 0 if both of its operands evaluate to 0. Otherwise, it produces 1.

*Example*:

| Operand A | !A |
|---|---|
| 0 | 1 |
| 1 | 0 |

| Operand A | Operand B | A\|\|B |
|---|---|---|
| 0 | 1 | 1 |
| 1 | 0 | 1 |
| 0 | 0 | 0 |
| 1 | 1 | 1 |

| Operand A | Operand B | A&&B |
|---|---|---|
| 0 | 1 | 0 |
| 1 | 0 | 0 |
| 0 | 0 | 0 |
| 1 | 1 | 1 |

Note that here we talk of zero and nonzero operands (not zero and 1). In general, any nonzero value can be used to represent the logical *true*, whereas only zero represents the logical *false*.

*The following are, therefore, all valid logical expressions*:

```
!20            //gives 0
10 && 5        //gives 1
10 || 5.5      //gives 1
10 && 0        //gives 0
```

C++ does not have a built-in boolean type. It is customary to use the type int for this purpose instead.

*For example*:

```
int sorted = 0;      //false
int balanced = 1;    //true
```

## BITWISE OPERATORS

C++ provides six bitwise operators for manipulating the individual bits in an integer quantity. These are summarized in table .

**Table. Bitwise Operators.**

| Operator | Name | Example | |
|---|---|---|---|
| ~ | Bitwise negation | ~'\011' | // gives '\366' |
| & | Bitwise and | '\011' & '\027' | // gives '\001' |
| \| | Bitwise or | '\011' \| '\027' | // gives '\037' |
| ^ | Bitwise exclusive Or | '\011' ^ '\027' | // gives '\036' |
| << | Bitwise left Shift | '\011' << 2 | // gives '\044' |
| >> | Bitwise right Shift | '\011' >> 2 | // gives '\002' |

Bitwise operators expect their operands to be integer quantities and treat them as bit sequences. Bitwise *negation* is a unary operator which reverses the bits in its operands. Bitwise *and* compares the corresponding bits of its operands and produces a 1 when both bits are 1, and 0 otherwise.

Bitwise *or* compares the corresponding bits of its operands and produces a 0 when both bits are 0, and 1 otherwise. Bitwise *exclusive or* compares the corresponding bits of its operands and produces a 0 when both bits are 1 or both bits are 0, and 1 otherwise.

Bitwise *left shift* operator and bitwise *right shift* operator both take a bit sequence as their left operand and a positive integer quantity *n* as their right operand. The former produces a bit sequence equal to the left operand but which has been shifted *n* bit positions to the left. The latter produces a bit sequence equal to the left operand but which has been shifted *n* bit positions to the right. Vacated bits at either end are set to 0.

To avoid worrying about the sign bit (which is machine dependent), it is common to declare a bit sequence as an unsigned quantity:

```
unsigned char x = '\011';
unsigned char y = '\027';
```

**Table. How the Bite are Calculate.**

| Example | Octal value | Bit Sequence | | | | | | | |
|---|---|---|---|---|---|---|---|---|---|
| x | 011 | 0 | 0 | 0 | 0 | 1 | 0 | 0 | 1 |
| y | 027 | 0 | 0 | 0 | 1 | 0 | 1 | 1 | 1 |
| ~x | 366 | 1 | 1 | 1 | 1 | 0 | 1 | 1 | 0 |

| | | | | | | | | | |
|---|---|---|---|---|---|---|---|---|---|
| x & y | 001 | 0 | 0 | 0 | 0 | 0 | 0 | 0 | 1 |
| x \| y | 037 | 0 | 0 | 0 | 1 | 1 | 1 | 1 | 1 |
| x ^ y | 036 | 0 | 0 | 0 | 1 | 1 | 1 | 1 | 0 |
| x << 2 | 044 | 0 | 0 | 1 | 0 | 0 | 1 | 0 | 0 |
| x >> 2 | 002 | 0 | 0 | 0 | 0 | 0 | 0 | 1 | 0 |

## INCREMENT/DECREMENT OPERATORS

The *auto increment* (++) and *auto decrement* (–) operators provide a convenient way of, respectively, adding and subtracting 1 from a numeric variable. These are summarized in Table. The examples assume the following variable definition:

```
int k = 5;
```

**Table. Increment and Decrement Operators.**

| Operator | Name | Example | |
|---|---|---|---|
| ++ | Auto Increment (prefix) | **++k + 10** | **//gives 16** |
| ++ | Auto Increment (postfix) | **k++ + 10** | **//gives 15** |
| - | Auto Decrement (prefix) | **–k + 10** | **//gives 14** |
| – | Auto Decrement (postfix) | **k– + 10** | **//gives 15** |

Both operators can be used in prefix and postfix form. The difference is significant. When used in prefix form, the operator is first applied and the outcome is then used in the expression. When used in the postfix form, the expression is evaluated first and then the operator applied.

## ASSIGNMENT OPERATOR

The assignment operator is used for storing a value at some memory location (typically denoted by a variable). Its left operand should be an lvalue, and its right operand may be an arbitrary expression. The latter is evaluated and the outcome is stored in the location denoted by the lvalue.

An lvalue (standing for left value) is anything that denotes a memory location in which a value may be stored. The only kind of lvalue we have seen so far in this book is a variable. The assignment operator has a number of variants, obtained by combining it with the arithmetic and bitwise operators. These are summarized in Table. The examples assume that n is an integer variable.

**Table Assignment Operators.**

| Operator | Example | Equivalent to |
|---|---|---|
| = | n = 25 | |
| += | n += 25 | n = n + 25 |
| -= | n -= 25 | n = n - 25 |
| *= | n *= 25 | n = n * 25 |
| /= | n /= 25 | n = n / 25 |
| %= | n %= 25 | n = n % 25 |
| &= | n &= 0xF2F2 | n = n & 0xF2F2 |
| = | n \|= 0xF2F2 | n = n \| 0xF2F2 |
| ^= | n ^= 0xF2F2 | n = n ^ 0xF2F2 |
| <<= | n <<= 4 | n = n << 4 |
| >>= | n >>= 4 | n = n >> 4 |

An assignment operation is itself an expression whose value is the value stored in its left operand. An assignment operation can therefore be used as the right operand of another assignment operation. Any number of assignments can be concatenated in this fashion to form one expression.

*For example*:

```
int m, n, p;
m = n = p = 100;          //means: n = (m =
   (p = 100));
m = (n = p = 100) + 2;    //means: m = (n =
   (p = 100)) + 2;
```

This is equally applicable to other forms of assignment.

*For example*:

```
m = 100;
m += n = p = 10; //means: m = m + (n = p =
   10);
```

## CONDITIONAL OPERATOR

The conditional operator takes three operands. It has the general form:

*operand1 ? operand2: operand3*

First *operand1* is evaluated, which is treated as a logical condition. If the result is nonzero then *operand2* is evaluated and its value is the final result. Otherwise, *operand3* is evaluated and its value is the final result. For example:

```
int m = 1, n = 2;
int min = (m < n ? m: n); //min receives 1
```

Note that of the second and the third operands of the conditional operator only one is evaluated. This may be significant when one or both contain side-effects (*i.e.*, their evaluation causes a change to the value of a variable). For example, in int min = (m < n ? m++: n++); m is incremented because m++ is evaluated but n is not incremented because n++ is not evaluated.

Because a conditional operation is itself an expression, it may be used as an operand of another conditional operation, that is, conditional expressions may be nested.

*For example*:

```
int m = 1, n = 2, p =3;
int min = (m < n ? (m < p ? m: p)
                 : (n < p ? n: p));
```

## COMMA OPERATOR

Multiple expressions can be combined into one expression using the comma operator. The comma operator takes two operands. It first evaluates the left operand and then the right operand, and returns the value of the latter as the finaloutcome.

*For example*:

```
int m, n, min;
int mCount = 0, nCount = 0;
//...
min = (m < n ? mCount++, m: nCount++, n);
```

Here when m is less than n, mCount++ is evaluated and the value of m is stored in min. Otherwise, nCount++ is evaluated and the value of n is stored in min.

## SIZE OF OPERATOR

C++ provides a useful operator, sizeof, for calculating the size of any data item or type. It takes a single operand which may be a type name (*e.g.*, int) or an expression (*e.g.*, 100) and returns the size of the specified entity in bytes. The outcome is totally machine-dependent. Listing 2.7 illustrates the use of sizeof on the built-in types we have encountered so far.

### Listing 2.7

```
#include <iostream.h>
int main (void)
{
    cout << "char   size = " << sizeof(char)
    << " bytes\n";
    cout << "char*  size = " << sizeof(char*)
    << " bytes\n";
    cout << "short  size = " << sizeof(short)
    << " bytes\n";
    cout << "int    size = " << sizeof(int)
    << " bytes\n";
    cout << "long   size = " << sizeof(long)
    << " bytes\n";
    cout << "float  size = " << sizeof(float)
    << " bytes\n";
    cout << "double size = " <<
    sizeof(double) << " bytes\n";
    cout << "1.55   size = " << sizeof(1.55)
    << " bytes\n";
    cout << "1.55L  size = " << sizeof(1.55L)
    << " bytes\n";
    cout << "HELLO  size = " <<
    sizeof("HELLO") << " bytes\n";
}
```

When run, the programme will produce the following output (on the author's PC):

```
char   size = 1 bytes
char*  size = 2 bytes
short  size = 2 bytes
int    size = 2 bytes
long   size = 4 bytes
float  size = 4 bytes
double size = 8 bytes
1.55   size = 8 bytes
```

```
1.55L  size = 10 bytes
HELLO  size = 6 bytes
```

## OPERATOR PRECEDENCE

The order in which operators are evaluated in an expression is significant and is determined by precedence rules. These rules divide the C++ operators into a number of precedence levels (see Table 2.9). Operators in higher levels take precedence over operators in lower levels.

## SIMPLE TYPE CONVERSION

A value in any of the built-in types we have see so far can be converted (*type-cast*) to any of the other types.

*For example*:

```
(int) 3.14                //converts 3.14 to an
   int to give 3
(long) 3.14               //converts 3.14 to a
   long to give 3L
(double) 2                //converts 2 to a
   double to give 2.0
(char) 122                //converts 122 to a
   char whose code is 122
(unsigned short) 3.14 //gives 3 as an
   unsigned short
```

As shown by these examples, the built-in type identifiers can be used as type operators. Type operators are unary (*i.e.*, take one operand) and appear inside brackets to the left of their operand.

This is called explicit type conversion. When the type name is just one word, an alternate notation may be used in which the brackets appear around the operand:

```
int(3.14)       //same as: (int) 3.14
```

In some cases, C++ also performs implicit type conversion. This happens when values of different types are mixed in an expression.

*For example*:

```
double  d = 1;    //d receives 1.0
int     i = 10.5; //i receives 10
```

```
i = i + d;     //means: i = int(double(i) +
  d)
```

In the last example, i + d involves mismatching types, so i is first converted to double (*promoted*) and then added to d. The result is a double which does not match the type of i on the left side of the assignment, so it is converted to int (*demoted*) before being assigned to i. The above rules represent some simple but common cases for type conversion.

## SIMPLE AND COMPOUND STATEMENTS

A simple statement is a computation terminated by a semicolon. Variable definitions and semicolon-terminated expressions are examples:

```
int i;             //declaration statement
++i;               //this has a side-effect
double d = 10.5;   //declaration statement
d + 5;             //useless statement!
```

The last example represents a useless statement, because it has no side-effect (d is added to 5 and the result is just discarded). The simplest statement is the null statement which consists of just a semicolon:

```
;          //null statement
```

Although the null statement has no side-effect, as we will see later in the chapter, it has some genuine uses. Multiple statements can be combined into a compound statement by enclosing them within braces.

*For example:*

```
{
   int min, i = 10, j = 20;
   min = (i < j ? i: j);
   cout << min << '\n';
}
```

*Compound statements are useful in two ways:*

- They allow us to put multiple statements in places where otherwise only single statements are allowed, and
- They allow us to introduce a new scope in the programme.

A scope is a part of the programme text within which a variable remains defined. For example, the scope of min, i, and j in the above example is from where they are defined till the closing brace of the compound statement.

Outside the compound statement, these variables are not defined. Because a compound statement may contain variable definitions and defines a scope for them, it is also called a block. The scope of a C++ variable is limited to the block immediately enclosing it.

## THE IF STATEMENT

It is sometimes desirable to make the execution of a statement dependent upon a condition being satisfied. The if statement provides a way of expressing this, the general form of which is:

```
if (exp ression)
{
    1.statement; ┐
    2.statement; │
    .            ├ Body of if statement
    .            │
    .            ┘
}
```

First *expression* is evaluated. If the condition is true then body of if *statement* is executed. Otherwise, nothing happens. For example, when dividing two values, we may want to check that the denominator is nonzero:

```
if (count != 0)
    average = sum/count;
```

To make multiple statements dependent on the same condition, we can use a compound statement:

```
if (balance > 0)
    {
    interest = balance * creditRate;
    balance += interest;
}
```

A variant form of the if statement allows us to specify two alternative statements: one which is executed if a condition is satisfied and one which is executed if the condition is *not* satisfied. This is called the if-else statement and has the general form:

```
if (expression)
{
    1.statement;  \
    2.statement;   |
    .              |  Body of if statement
    .              |
    .             /
}

else
{
    1.statement;  \
    2.statement;   |
    .              |  Body of else part
    .              |
    .             /
}
```

First *expression* is evaluated. If the outcome is nonzero then body of if is executed. Otherwise, else part is executed.

*For example*:

```
if (balance > 0)
{
   interest = balance * creditRate;
   balance += interest;
} else
{
   interest = balance * debitRate;
```

```
    balance += interest;
}
```

Given the similarity between the two alternative parts, the whole statement can be simplified to:

```
if (balance > 0)
    interest = balance * creditRate;
else
    interest = balance * debitRate;
    balance += interest;
```

Or simplified even further using a conditional expression:

```
interest = balance * (balance > 0 ?
    creditRate: debitRate);
balance += interest;
```

Or just:

```
balance += balance * (balance > 0 ?
    creditRate: debitRate);
```

If statements may be nested by having an if statement appear inside another if statement.

*For example*:

```
/*Find greatest number among given three
    number*/
#include<iostream.h>
#include<conio.h>
main()
{
    int a,b,c;
    cout<<"Enter value for a: ";
    cin>>a;
    cout<<"Enter value for b: ";
    cin>>b;
    cout<<"Enter value for c: ";
    cin>>c;
    if(a>b)
    {
          if(a>c)
          {
                cout<<"a is greatest";
          }
```

```
        }
        else
        {
                if(b>a)
                {
                        if(b>c)
                        {
                                cout<<"b is greatest";
                        }
                }
                else
                {
                        cout<<"c is greatest";
                }
        }
    }
```

***Output:***

Ente value for a:5
Ente value for b:6
Ente value for c:2
b is greatest

## ELSE IF STATEMENT

Else if statement is an multidicision making statement. In the statement first condition is checked. If condition is true then action will be taken. Otherwise further next condition will be checked and this process will continue till the end of execution. For example

```
if (ch >= '0' && ch <= '9')
   kind = digit;
else{
   if (cha >= 'A' && ch <= 'Z')
      kind = capitalLetter;
   else{
      if (ch >= 'a' && ch <= 'z')
         kind = smallLetter;
      else
         kind = special;
```

```
        }
    }
```

## THE SWITCH STATEMENT

The switch statement provides a way of choosing between a set of alternatives, based on the value of an expression. The general form of the switch statement is:

```
switch (expression)
{
    case constant1:
            statements;
    break;
    ...
    case constantn:
            statements;
    break;
            default:
    statements;
}
```

First *expression* (called the switch tag) is evaluated, and the outcome is compared to each of the numeric *constants* (called case labels), in the order they appear, until a match is found. The *statements* following the matching case are then executed. Note the plural: each case may be followed by zero or more statements (not just one statement). Execution continues until either a break statement is encountered or all intervening statements until the end of the switch statement are executed. The final default case is optional and is exercised if none of the earlier cases provide a match.

For example, suppose we have parsed a binary arithmetic operation into its three components and stored these in variables operator, operand1, and operand2. The following switch statement performs the operation and stored the result in result.

```
#include<iostream.h>
Void main()
{
    char operator;
```

```
    cout<<"Enter operator:";
    cin>>operator;
    switch (operator)
    {
        case '+':
            result = operand1 + operand2;
            cout<<"Result: "<<result;
            break;
        case '-':
            result = operand1 - operand2;
            cout<<"Result: "<<result;
            break;
        case '*':
            result = operand1 * operand2;
            cout<<"Result: "<<result;
            break;
        case '/':
            result = operand1 / operand2;
            break;
        default:
            cout << "unknown operator: " <<
   ch << '\n';
            break;
        }
}
```

As illustrated by this example, it is usually necessary to include a break statement at the end of each case. The break terminates the switch statement by jumping to the very end of it. There are, however, situations in which it makes sense to have a case without a break.

For example, if we extend the above statement to also allow x to be used as a multiplication operator, we will have:

```
switch (operator) {
   case '+':   result = operand1 + operand2;
               break;
   case '-':   result = operand1 - operand2;
               break;
   case 'x':
```

```
    case '*':     result = operand1 * operand2;
                  break;
    case '/':     result = operand1 / operand2;
                  break;
    default:      cout << "unknown operator: "
    << ch << '\n';
    break;
}
```

Because case 'x' has no break statement (in fact no statement at all!), when this case is satisfied, execution proceeds to the statements of the next case and the multiplication is performed.

It should be obvious that any switch statement can also be written as multiple if-else statements. The above statement, for example, may be written as:

```
if (operator == '+')
    result = operand1 + operand2;
else if (operator == '-')
    result = operand1 - operand2;
else if (operator == 'x' || operator == '*')
    result = operand1 * operand2;
else if (operator == '/')
    result = operand1/operand2;
else
    cout << "unknown operator: " << ch <<
    '\n';
```

However, the switch version is arguably neater in this case. In general, preference should be given to the switch version when possible. The if-else approach should be reserved for situation where a switch cannot do the job (*e.g.*, when the conditions involved are not simple equality expressions, or when the case labels are not numeric constants).

## WHILE STATEMENT

The while statement (also called while loop) provides a way of repeating an statement while a condition holds. It is one of the three flavours of iteration in C++.

*The general form of the while statement is:*

```
while (exp ression)
{
    1.statement;\
                 } body of while loop
    2.statement;/
}
```

First *expression* (called the loop condition) is evaluated. If the outcome is nonzero then *statement* (called the loop body) is executed and the whole process is repeated. Otherwise, the loop is terminated.

*For example*:

```
/*Programme to create table of given number
  using while loop*/
#include<iostream.h>
#include<conio.h>
void main()
{
   int mul,i=1,n;
   cout<<"Enter the value for n: ";
   cin>>n;
   while(i<=10)
   {
        mul=i*n;
        cout<<i<<"*"<<n<<"="<<mul<<endl;
        i++;
   }
}
```

It is not unusual for a while loop to have an empty body (*i.e.*, a null statement).

The following loop, for example, sets n to its greatest odd factor.

```
while (n % 2 == 0 && n/= 2)
   ;
```

Here the loop condition provides all the necessary computation, so there is no real need for a body. The loop condition not only tests that n is even, it also divides n by two and ensures that the loop will terminate should n be zero.

## THE DO STATEMENT

The do statement (also called do loop) is similar to the while statement, except that its body is executed first and then the loop condition is examined. The general form of the do statement is:

```
{
    1.statement;
                  } body of do while loop
    2.statement;
}while(exp ression);
```

First *statement* is executed and then *expression* is evaluated. If the outcome of the latter is nonzero then the whole process is repeated. Otherwise, the loop is terminated.

The do loop is less frequently used than the while loop. It is useful for situations where we need the loop body to be executed at least once, regardless of the loop condition.

For example, suppose we wish to repeatedly read a value and print its square, and stop when the value is zero. This can be expressed as the following loop:

```
do {
    cin >> n;
    cout << n * n << '\n';
} while (n != 0);
```

Unlike the while loop, the do loop is never used in situations where it would have a null body. Although a do loop with a null body would be equivalent to a similar while loop, the latter is always preferred for its superior readability.

## FOR STATEMENT

The for statement (also called for loop) is similar to the while statement, but has two additional components: an expression which is evaluated only once before everything else, and an expression which is evaluated once at the end of each iteration. The general form of the for statement is:

```
for (expression1; expression2; expression3)
    statement;
```

First *expression1* is evaluated. Each time round the loop, *expression2* is evaluated. If the outcome is nonzero then statement is executed and *expression3* is evaluated. Otherwise, the loop is terminated. The general for loop is equivalent to the following while loop:

```
expression1;
while (expression2) {
   statement;
   expression3;
}
```

The most common use of for loops is for situations where a variable is incremented or decremented with every iteration of the loop. The following for loop, for example, calculates the sum of all integers from 1 to n.

```
sum = 0;
for (i = 1; i <= n; ++i)
     sum += i;
```

This is preferred to the while-loop version we saw earlier. In this example, i is usually called the loop variable.

C++ allows the first expression in a for loop to be a variable definition. In the above loop, for example, i can be defined inside the loop itself:

```
for (int i = 1; i <= n; ++i)
     sum += i;
```

Contrary to what may appear, the scope for i is *not* the body of the loop, but the loop itself. Scope-wise, the above is equivalent to:

```
int i;
for (i = 1; i <= n; ++i)
     sum += i;
```

Any of the three expressions in a for loop may be empty.

For example, removing the first and the third expression gives us something identical to a while loop:

```
for (; i != 0;)        //is equivalent to:
   while (i != 0)
    something;         //something;
```

Removing all the expressions gives us an infinite loop. This loop's condition is assumed to be always true:

```
for (;;)               //infinite loop
     something;
```

For loops with multiple loop variables are not unusual. In such cases, the comma operator is used to separate their expressions:

```
for (i = 0, j = 0; i + j < n; ++i, ++j)
    something;
```

Because loops are statements, they can appear inside other loops. In other words, loops can be nested.

*For example*:

```
for (int i = 1; i <= 3; ++i)
   for (int j = 1; j <= 3; ++j)
         cout << '(' << i << ',' << j <<
   ")\n";
```

produces the product of the set {1,2,3} with itself, giving the output:

(1,1)
(1,2)
(1,3)
(2,1)
(2,2)
(2,3)
(3,1)
(3,2)
(3,3)

*Example*: Programme to display following output if n=3 using for loop

```
  *
 ***
*****
 ***
  *
```

```
#include<iostream.h>
main()
{
   int n,i,j,a,b;
   cout<<"Enter the value of n:";
   cin>>n;
   for(i=1;i<=n;i++)
   {
```

```
            a=i;
            b=n-1;
            for(j=1;j<=i;j++)
            {
                  cout<<"a "<<t;
                  b—;
                  a=a+b;
            }
            cout<<'\n';
      }
   }
```

*Example*: Programme to display following output if n=4 using for loop

```
1
232
34543
4567654
```

```
   #include<iostream.h>
   main()
   {
      int n,i,j,a,b;
      cout<<"Enter the value of n:";
      cin>>n;
      a=2;
      for(i=1;i<=n;i++)
      {
            for(j=i;j<=n;j++)
            {
                  cout<<" ";
            }
            for(j=i;j<=a*i-1;j++)
            {
                  cout<<j;
            }
            for(j=a*i-2;j>=i;j—)
            {
                  cout<<j;
            }
```

```
            cout<<"\n";
        }
    }
```

*Example*: Programme to display following output if n=4 using for loop

```
1
1 1
1 1 1
1 1 1 1
```

```
#include<iostream.h>
main()
{
    int n,i,j,a,b;
    cout<<"Enter the value of n:";
    cin>>n;
    for(i=1;i<=n;i++)
    {
            for(j=i;j<=n;j++)
            {
                    cout<<" ";
            }
            for(j=1;j<=2*i-1;j++)
            {
                    if(j%2==0)
                            cout<<" ";
                    else
                            cout<<"1";
            }
            cout<<"\n";
    }
}
```

## CONTINUE STATEMENT

The continue statement terminates the current iteration of a loop and instead jumps to the next iteration. It applies to the loop immediately enclosing the continue statement. It is an error to use the continue statement outside a loop. In while and do loops, the next iteration commences from the loop condition. In a for loop, the next iteration commences from the loop's third expression. For example, a loop which repeatedly reads in a number, processes it but ignores negative numbers, and terminates when the number is zero, may be expressed as:

```
do {
   cin >> num;
   if (num < 0) continue;
   //process num here...
} while (num != 0);
```

*This is equivalent to*:

```
do {
   cin >> num;
   if (num >= 0) {
        //process num here...
   }
} while (num != 0);
```

A variant of this loop which reads in a number exactly *n* times (rather than until the number is zero) may be expressed as:

```
for (i = 0; i < n; ++i) {
   cin >> num;
   if (num < 0) continue;         //causes a
   jump to: ++i
   //process num here...
}
```

When the continue statement appears inside nested loops, it applies to the loop immediately enclosing it, and not to the outer loops. For example, in the following set of nested loops, the continue applies to the for loop, and not the while loop:

```
while (more) {
   for (i = 0; i < n; ++i) {
        cin >> num;
        if (num < 0) continue;       /   /
   causes a jump to: ++i
        //process num here...
   }
   //etc...
}
```

## BREAK STATEMENT

A break statement may appear inside a loop (while, do, or for) or a switch statement. It causes a jump out of these constructs, and hence terminates them. Like the continue statement, a break statement only applies to the loop or switch immediately enclosing it. It is an error to use the break statement outside a loop or a switch. For example, suppose we wish to read in a user password, but would like to allow the user a limited number of attempts:

```
for (i = 0; i < attempts; ++i)
{
   cout << "Please enter your password: ";
   cin >> password;
   if (Verify(password)) //check password
   for correctness
        break;             //drop out of the
   loop
   cout << "Incorrect!\n";
}
```

Here we have assumed that there is a function called Verify which checks a password and returns true if it is correct, and false otherwise. Rewriting the loop without a break statement is always possible by using an additional logical variable (verified) and adding it to the loop condition:

```
verified = 0;
for (i = 0; i < attempts && !verified; ++i)
{
   cout << "Please enter your password: ";
   cin >> password;
   verified = Verify(password));
   if (!verified)
        cout << "Incorrect!\n";
}
```

The break version is arguably simpler and therefore preferred.

## GOTO STATEMENT

The goto statement provides the lowest-level of jumping.

It has the general form: goto label; where *label* is an identifier which marks the jump destination of goto. The label should be followed by a colon and appear before a statement within the same function as the goto statement itself.

For example, the role of the break statement in the for loop in the previous section can be emulated by a goto:

```
for (i = 0; i < attempts; ++i)
{
        cout << "Please enter your password:
";
        cin >> password;
        if (Verify(password))  //check
password for correctness
            goto out;          //drop out
of the loop
        cout << "Incorrect!\n";
}
out:
   //etc...
```

Because goto provides a free and unstructured form of jumping (unlike break and continue), it can be easily misused. Most programmers these days avoid using it altogether in favour of clear programming. Nevertheless, goto does have some legitimate (though rare) uses. Because of the potential complexity of such cases, furnishing of examples is postponed to the later parts of the book.

## RETURN STATEMENT

The return statement enables a function to return a value to its caller. It has the general form: return *expression*; where *expression* denotes the value returned by the function. The type of this value should match the return type of the function. For a function whose return type is void, *expression* should be empty: return;

The only function we have discussed so far is main, whose return type is always int. The return value of main is what the programme returns to the operating system when it completes its execution.

Under UNIX, for example, it its conventional to return 0 from main when the programme executes without errors. Otherwise, a non-zero error code is returned. For example:

```
int main (void)
{
   cout << "Hello World\n";
   return 0;
}
```

When a function has a non-void return value (as in the above example), failing

to return a value will result in a compiler warning. The actual return value will be undefined in this case (*i.e.*, it will be whatever value which happens to be in its corresponding memory location at the time).

# 3

# Functions

## FUNCTION NAME

The function parameters (also called its signature). This is a set of zero or more typed identifiers used for passing values to and from the function.? The function return type. This specifies the type of value the function returns. A function which returns nothing should have the return type void. The body of a function contains the computational steps (statements) that comprise the function. Using a function involves 'calling' it. A function call consists of the function name followed by the call operator brackets '()', inside which zero or more comma-separated arguments appear. The number of arguments should match the number of function parameters.

Each argument is an expression whose type should match the type of the corresponding parameter in the function interface. When a function call is executed, the arguments are first evaluated and their resulting values are assigned to the corresponding parameters.

The function body is then executed. Finally, the function return value (if any) is passed to the caller. Since a call to a function whose return type is non-void yields a return value, the call is an expression and may be used in other expressions. By contrast, a call to a function whose return type is void is a statement. In c++, basically there are two type of functions *i.e.* Library function and User defined functions. Library function are those which already exist in the library of c++ like pow(), sqrt() etc. User defined function are those which is defined by the programmer. User defined function are three types as follows. Function with no arguments and no return value : In this type there will not be pass any argument through function and not recieve any value. For Example:

```
  #include<iostream.h>
2 void main()
  {
3    void sum() ;
4    sum() ;
  }
5 void sum()
  {
     int number1,number2,addition ;
7    cout<< "Enter the value of number1,
     number2 :";
     cin>> number1>>number2 ;
     addition= number1+number2 ;
     cout<< "ADDITION OF TWO NUMBER IS
     "<<addition;
  }
```

## ANNOTATION

1-3 These lines are same as previous example

4. This line defines to declare the user defined function sum() with return type void (not return any value)
5. This line calling the function sum() (means control will transfer on the definition of function)
7. This line defines the function interface. It starts with the return type of the function (void in this case). After execution of the body of function control again pass to the same address from which it transfer and then further statements executed
2. Function with arguments and no return value : In this type, some parameter is pass as argument through function and not receive any value.

*For example*:

```
#include<iostream.h>
void main()
```

```
3 {
4     int power (int , int);
5     int base,exponent;
6     cout<<"Enter base & exponent";
7     cin>>base>>exponent;
8     power(base,exponent); //base & exponent
      are actual parameter
9 }
10 int Power (int base, int exponent) /*base &
      exponent are
   formal parameter*/
11    {
12          int result = 1;
13          for (int i = 0; i < exponent; ++i)
14                result *= base;
15          cout<<result;
16 }
```

## ANNOTATION

1-9 These lines are same as previous example

10. This line defines the function interface. It starts with the return type of the function (int in this case). The function name appears next followed by its parameter list. Power has two parameters (base and exponent) which are of types int and int, respectively Note that the syntax for parameters is similar to the syntax for defining variables: type identifier followed by the parameter name. However, it is *not* possible to follow a type identifier with multiple comma-separated parameters: int Power (int base, exponent)//Wrong!

11. This brace marks the beginning of the function body.

12. This line is a local variable definition.

13-14 This for-loop raises base to the power of exponent and stores the outcome in result.

15 This line display the result.

16 This brace marks the end of the function body.

3. Function with arguments and return value : In this

type, some parameter is pass as argument through function and not receive any value.

*For example*:

```
1  #include<iostream.h>
2  void main()
3  {
4      int power (int, int);
5      int base,exponent;
6      cout<<"Enter base & exponent";
7      cin>>base>>exponent;
8      cout<<power(base,exponent);
9  }
10     int Power (int base, int exponent)
11     {
12     int result = 1;
13     for (int i = 0; i < exponent; ++i)
14           result *= base;
15     return(result);
15 }
```

## ANNOTATION

1-9. These lines are same as previous example

10. This line defines the function interface. It starts with the return type of the function (int in this case). The function name appears next followed by its parameter list. Power has two parameters (base and exponent) which are of types int and int, respectively Note that the syntax for parameters is similar to the syntax for defining variables: type identifier followed by the parameter name. However, it is *not* possible to follow a type dentifier with multiple comma-separated parameters: int Power (int base, exponent)//Wrong!

11. This brace marks the beginning of the function body.

12. This line is a local variable definition.

13-14 This for-loop raises base to the power of exponent and stores the outcome n result.

15 This line display the result.

16 This brace marks the end of the function body.

Listing 4.9 illustrates how this function is called. The effect of this call is that first the argument values 2 and 4 are, respectively, assigned to the parameters base and exponent, and then the function body is evaluated.

**Listing 4.9**

```
#include <iostream.h>
main (void)
{
    cout << "2 ^ 8 = " << Power(2,8) << '\n';
}
When run, this programme will produce the
    following output:
2 ^ 8 = 256
```

In general, a function should be declared before its is used. A function declaration simply consists of the function prototype, which specifies the function name, parameter types, and return type. Line 2 in Listing 4.10 shows how Power may be declared for the above programme. Although a function may be declared without its parameter names, int power (int, unsigned int); this is not recommended unless the role of the parameters is obvious..

**Listing 4.10**

```
1  #include <iostream.h>
2  int power (int base, unsigned int exponent);/
       /function declaration
3  main (void)
4  {
5      cout << "2 ^ 8 = " << Power(2,8) << '\n';
6  }
7  int power (int base, unsigned int exponent)
8  {
9      int result = 1;
10     for (int i = 0; i < exponent; ++i)
11         result *= base;
```

```
    return result;
}
```

Because a function definition contains a prototype, it also serves as a declaration. Therefore if the definition of a function appears before its use, no additional declaration is needed.

Use of function prototypes is nevertheless encouraged for all circumstances. Collecting these in a separate header file enables other programmers to quickly access the functions without having to read their entire definitions.

## PARAMETERS AND ARGUMENTS

C++ supports two styles of parameters: value and reference. A value parameter receives a *copy* of the value of the argument passed to it. As a result, if the function makes any changes to the parameter, this will not affect the argument.

*For example, in:*

```
#include <iostream.h>
void Foo (int num)
{
    num = 0;
    cout << "num = " << num << '\n';
}
int main (void)
{
    int x = 10;
    Foo(x);
    cout << "x = " << x << '\n';
    return 0;
}
```

The single parameter of Foo is a value parameter. As far as this function is concerned, num behaves just like a local variable inside the function.

When the function is called and x passed to it, num receives a copy of the value of x. As aresult, although num is set to 0 by the function, this does not affect x. The programme produces the following output:

```
num = 0;
x = 10;
```

A reference parameter, on the other hand, receives the argument passed to it and works on it directly. Any changes made by the function to a reference parameter is in effect directly applied to the argument.

Within the context of function calls, the two styles of passing arguments are, respectively, called pass-by-value and pass-by-reference. It is perfectly valid for a function to use pass-by-value for some of its parameters and pass-by-reference for others. The former is used much more often in practice.

## GLOBAL AND LOCAL SCOPE

Everything defined at the programme scope level (*i.e.*, outside main functions and classes) is said to have a global scope. Thus the sample functions we have seen so far all have a global scope. Variables may also be defined at the global scope:

```
int year = 1994;      //global variable
int Max (int, int); //global function
int main (void)      //global function
{
   //...
}
```

Uninitialized global variables are automatically initialized to zero. Since global entities are visible at the programme level, they must also be unique at the programme level. This means that the same global variable or function may not be *defined* more than once at the global level. (However, as we will see later, a function name may be reused so long as its signature remains unique.) Global entities are generally accessible everywhere in the programme.

Each block in a programme defines a local scope. Thus the body of a function represents a local scope. The parameters of a function have the same scope as the function body. Variables defined within a local scope are visible to that scope only. Hence, a variable need only be unique within its own scope. Local scopes may be nested, in which case the inner scopes override the outer scopes. For example, in

```
int xyz;                    //xyz is global
void Foo (int xyz)  //xyz is local to the
```

```
   body of Foo
{
   if (xyz > 0) {
         double xyz; //xyz is local to this
   block
         //...
   }
}
```

there are three distinct scopes, each containing a distinct xyz. Generally, the lifetime of a variable is limited to its scope. So, for example, global variables last for the duration of programme execution, while local variables are created when their scope is entered and destroyed when their scope is exited.

The memory space for global variables is reserved *prior* to programme execution commencing, whereas the memory space for local variables is allocated on the fly *during* programme execution.

## SCOPE OPERATOR

Because a local scope overrides the global scope, having a local variable with the same name as a global variable makes the latter inaccessible to the local scope. For example, in

```
int error;
void Error (int error)
{
   //...
}
```

The global error is inaccessible inside Error, because it is overridden by the local error parameter. This problem is overcome using the unary scope operator:: which takes a global entity as argument:

```
int error;
void Error (int error)
{
   //...
   if (::error != 0)//refers to global error
         //...
}
```

## AUTO VARIABLES

Because the lifetime of a local variable is limited and is determined automatically, these variables are also called automatic. The storage class specifier auto may be used to explicitly specify a local variable to be automatic. For example:

```
void Foo (void)
{
    auto int xyz;      //same as: int xyz;
    //...
}
```

This is rarely used because all local variables are by default automatic.

## REGISTER VARIABLES

As mentioned earlier, variables generally denote memory locations where variable values are stored. When the programme code refers to a variable (*e.g.*, in an expression), the compiler generates machine code which accesses the memory location denoted by the variable. For frequently-used variables (*e.g.*, loop variables), efficiency gains can be obtained by keeping the variable in a register instead thereby avoiding memory access for that variable.

The storage class specifier register may be used to indicate to the compiler that the variable should be stored in a register if possible. For example:

```
for (register int i = 0; i < n; ++i)
    sum += i;
```

Here, each time round the loop, i is used three times: once when it is compared to n, once when it is added to sum, and once when it is incremented. Therefore it makes sense to keep i in a register for the duration of the loop. Note that register is only a *hint* to the compiler, and in some cases the compiler may choose not to use a register when it is asked to do so. One reason for this is that any machine has a limited number of registers and it may be the case that they are all in use.

Even when the programmer does not use register declarations, many optimizing compilers try to make an intelligent guess and use registers where they are likely to improve the performance of the programme. Use of register declarations can be left as an after thought; they can always be added later by reviewing the code and inserting it in appropriate places.

## STATIC VARIABLES AND FUNCTIONS

It is often useful to confine the accessibility of a global variable or function to a single file. This is facilitated by the storage class specifier static. For example, consider a puzzle game programme which consists of three files for game generation, game solution, and user interface.

The game solution file would contain a Solve function and a number of other functions ancillary to Solve. Because the latter are only for the private use of Solve, it is best not to make them accessible outside the file:

```
static int FindNextRoute (void) / / o n l y
    accessible in this file
{
    //...
}
//...
int Solve (void)                    /         /
    accessible outside this file
{
    //...
}
```

The same argument may be applied to the global variables in this file that are for the private use of the functions in the file. For example, a global variable which records the length of the shortest route so far is best defined as static:

```
static int shortestRoute;//static global
    variable
```

A local variable in a function may also be defined as static. The variable will remain only accessible within its local scope; however, its lifetime will no longer be confined to this scope, but will instead be global. In other words, a static local variable is a global variable which is only accessible within its local scope. Static local variables are useful when we want the value of a local variable to persist across the calls to the function in which it appears. For example, consider an Error function which keeps a count of the errors and aborts the programme when the count exceeds a preset limit:

```
void Error (char *message)
{
    static int count = 0; //static local
    variable
    if (++count > limit)
        Abort();
    //...
}
```

Like global variables, static local variables are automatically initialized to 0.

## EXTERN VARIABLES AND FUNCTIONS

Because a global variable may be defined in one file and referred to in other files, some means of telling the compiler that the variable is defined elsewhere may be needed. Otherwise, the compiler may object to the variable as undefined. This is facilitated by an extern declaration. For example, the declaration

```
extern int size;    //variable declaration
```

informs the compiler that size is actually defined somewhere (may be later in this file or in another file). This is called a variable declaration (not definition) because it does not lead to any storage being allocated for size.

It is a poor programming practice to include an initializer for an extern variable, since this causes it to become a variable definition and have storage allocated for it:

```
extern int size = 10;    //no longer a
    declaration!
```

If there is another definition for size elsewhere in the programme, it will eventually clash with this one. Function prototypes may also be declared as extern, but this has no effect when a prototype appears at the global scope. It is more useful for declaring function prototypes inside a function. For example:

```
double Tangent (double angle)
{
   extern double sin(double);  //defined
   elsewhere
   extern double cos(double);  //defined
   elsewhere
   return sin(angle)/cos(angle);
}
```

The best place for extern declarations is usually in header files so that they can be easily included and shared by source files.

## SYMBOLIC CONSTANTS

Preceding a variable definition by the keyword const makes that variable readonly (*i.e.*, a symbolic constant). A constant must be initialized to some value when it is defined.

*For example*:

```
const int          maxSize = 128;
const double  pi = 3.141592654;
```

Once defined, the value of a constant cannot be changed:

```
maxSize = 256;        //illegal!
```

A constant with no type specifier is assumed to be of type int:

```
const maxSize = 128;      //maxSize is of
   type int
```

With pointers, two aspects need to be considered: the pointer itself, and the object pointed to, either of which or both can be constant:

```
const char *str1 = "pointer to constant";
char *const str2 = "constant pointer";
const char *const str3 = "constant pointer
   to constant";
str1[0] = 'P';                   //illegal!
str1 = "ptr to const";           //ok
str2 = "const ptr";              //illegal!
str2[0] = 'P';                   //ok
str3 = "const to const ptr";     //illegal!
str3[0] = 'C';                   //illegal!
```

A function parameter may also be declared to be constant. This may be used to indicate that the function does not change the value of a parameter: int Power (const int base, const unsigned int exponent)

```
{
    //...
}
```

A function may also return a constant result: const char* SystemVersion (void)

```
{
    return "5.2.1";
}
```

The usual place for constant definition is within header files so that they can be shared by source files.

## ENUMERATIONS

An enumeration of symbolic constants is introduced by an enum declaration. This is useful for declaring a set of closely-related constants.

For example,

```
enum {north, south, east, west};
```

introduces four enumerators which have integral values starting from 0 (*i.e.*, north is 0, south is 1, etc.) Unlike symbolic constants, however, which are readonly variables, enumerators have no allocated memory.

The default numbering of enumerators can be overruled by explicit initialization:

```
enum {north = 10, south, east = 0, west};
```

Here, south is 11 and west is 1.

An enumeration can also be named, where the name becomes a user-defined

type. This is useful for defining variables which can only be assigned a limited set of values. For example, in

```
enum Direction {north, south, east, west};
Direction d;
```

d can only be assigned one of the enumerators for Direction. Enumerations are particularly useful for naming the cases of a switch statement.

```
switch (d) {
   case north://...
   case south://...
   case east://...
   case west://...
}
```

We will extensively use the following enumeration for representing boolean values in the programmes in this book:

```
enum Bool {false, true};
```

## RUNTIME STACK

Like many other modern programming languages, C++ function call execution is based on a runtime stack. When a function is called, memory space is allocated on this stack for the function parameters, return value, and local variables, as well as a local stack area for expression evaluation.

The allocated space is called a stack frame. When a function returns, the allocated stack frame is released so that it can be reused. For example, consider a situation where main calls a function called Solve which in turn calls another function called Normalize:

```
int Normalize (void)
{
   //...
}
int Solve (void)
{
   //...
   Normalize();
   //...
}
int main (void)
{
   //...
   Solve();
   //...
}
```

| Main | Solve | Normalize |
|---|---|---|

It is important to note that the calling of a function involves the overheads of creating a stack frame for it and removing the stack frame when it returns. For most functions, this overhead is negligible compared to the actual computation the function performs.

## INLINE FUNCTIONS

Suppose that a programme frequently requires to find the absolute value of an integer quantity. For a value denoted by n, this may be expressed as:

```
(n > 0 ? n: -n)
```

However, instead of replicating this expression in many places in the programme, it is better to define it as a function:

```
int Abs (int n)
{
    return n > 0 ? n: -n;
}
```

The function version has a number of advantages. First, it leads to a more

readable programme. Second, it is reusable. And third, it avoid undesirable sideeffects when the argument is itself an expression with side-effects.

The disadvantage of the function version, however, is that its frequent use can lead to a considerable performance penalty due to the overheads associated with calling a function. For example, if Abs is used within a loop which is iterated thousands of times, then it will have an impact on performance. The overhead can be avoided by defining Abs as an inline function:

```
inline int Abs (int n)
{
    return n > 0 ? n: -n;
}
```

The effect of this is that when Abs is called, the compiler, instead of generating code to call Abs, expands and substitutes the body of Abs in place of the call. While essentially the same computation is performed, no function call is involved and hence no stack frame is allocated. Because calls to an inline function are expanded, no trace of the function itself will be left in the compiled code.

Therefore, if a function is defined inline in one file, it may not be available to other files. Consequently, inline functions are commonly placed in header files so that they can be shared.

Like the register keyword, inline is a *hint* which the compiler is not obliged to observe. Generally, the use of inline should be restricted to simple, frequently used functions. A function which contains anything more than a couple of statements is unlikely to be a good candidate. Use of inline for excessively long and complex functions is almost certainly ignored by the compiler.

## RECURSION

A function which calls itself is said to be recursive. Recursion is a general programming technique applicable to problems which can be defined in terms of themselves. Take the factorial problem, for instance, which is defined as:

- Factorial of 0 is 1.
- Factorial of a positive number *n* is *n* times the factorial of *n*-1.

The second line clearly indicates that factorial is defined in terms of itself and hence can be expressed as a recursive function with example:

```
#include<iostream.h>
void main()
{
   int factorial(unsigned int);
   unsigned int n;
   cout<<"Enter the value for n: ";
   cin>>n;
   cout<<factorial(n);
}
int factorial(unsigned int n)
{
   return n==0 ? 1: n * factorial(n-1);
}
```

For n set to 3, Table 4.11 provides a trace of the calls to Factorial. The stack frames for these calls appear sequentially on the runtime stack, one after the other.

**Table. Factorial(3) Execution Trace.**

| Call | n | n == 0 | n * Factorial(n-1) | Returns |
|---|---|---|---|---|
| First | 3 | 0 | 3 * Factorial(2) | 6 |
| Second | 2 | 0 | 2 * Factorial(1) | 2 |
| Third | 1 | 0 | 1 * Factorial(0) | 1 |
| Fourth | 0 | 1 | 1 | 1 |

A recursive function must have at least one termination condition which can be satisfied. Otherwise, the function will call itself indefinitely until the runtime stack overflows.

The Factorial function, for example, has the termination condition n == 0 which, when satisfied, causes the recursive calls to fold back. (Note that for a negative n this condition will never be satisfied and Factorial will fail).

As a general rule, all recursive functions can be rewritten using iteration. In situations where the number of stack frames involved may be quite large, the iterative version is preferred. In other cases, the elegance and simplicity of the recursive version may give it the edge.

For factorial, for example, a very large argument will lead to as many stack frames. An iterative version is therefore preferred in this case:

```
int Factorial (unsigned int n)
{
    int result = 1;
    while (n > 0) result *= n–;
    return result;
}
```

## DEFAULT ARGUMENTS

Default argument is a programming convenience which removes the burden of having to specify argument values for all of a function's parameters. For example, consider a function for reporting errors:

```
void Error (char *message, int severity =
    0);
```

Here, severity has a default argument of 0; both the following calls are therefore,
valid:

```
Error("Division by zero", 3);   //severity
    set to 3
Error("Round off error");       //severity
    set to 0
```

As the first call illustrates, a default argument may be overridden by explicitly specifying an argument. Default arguments are suitable for situations where certain (or all) function parameters frequently take the same values. In Error, for example, severity 0 errors are more common than others and therefore a good candidate for default argument. A less appropriate use of default arguments would be:

```
int Power (int base, unsigned int exponent =
    1);
```

Because 1 (or any other value) is unlikely to be a frequently-used one in this situation. To avoid ambiguity, all default arguments must be trailing arguments. The following declaration is therefore illegal:

```
void Error (char *message = "Bomb", int
    severity);//Illegal!
```

A default argument need not necessarily be a constant. Arbitrary expressions can be used, so long as the variables used in the expression are available to the scope of the function definition (*e.g.*, global variables).

The accepted convention for default arguments is to specify them in function declarations, not function definitions. Because function declarations appear in header files, this enables the user of a function to have control over the default arguments. Thus different default arguments can be specified for different situations. It is, however, illegal to specify two different default arguments for the same function in a file.

## VARIABLE NUMBER OF ARGUMENTS

It is sometimes desirable, if not necessary, to have functions which take a variable number of arguments. A simple example is a function which takes a set of menu options as arguments, displays the menu, and allows the user to choose one of theoptions. To be general, the function should be able to accept any number of options as arguments. This may be expressed as,

```
int Menu (char *option1...);
```

which states that Menu should be given one argument or more. Menu can access its arguments using a set of macro definitions in the header file stdarg.h, as illustrated by Listing 4.11. The relevant macros are highlighted in bold.

## Listing 4.11

```
1  #include <iostream.h>
2  #include <stdarg.h>
3  int Menu (char *option1...)
4  {
5     va_list args;                         //argument list
6     char* option = option1;
7     int   count = 0, choice = 0;
8     va_start(args, option1);              // initialize args
9     do {
10           cout << ++count << ". " << option << '\n';
11    } while ((option = va_arg(args, char*)) != 0);
12    va_end(args);                         //clean up args
13    cout << "option? ";
14    cin >> choice;
15    return (choice > 0 && choice <= count) ? choice: 0;
16 }
```

### Annotation

5 To access the arguments, args is declared to be of type va_list.

8 Args is initialized by calling va_start. The second argument to va_start must be the last function parameter explicitly declared in the function header.

11 Subsequent arguments are retrieved by calling va_arg. The second argument to va_arg must be the expected type of that argument (*i.e.,* char* here). For this technique to work, the last argument must be a 0, marking the end of the argument list. Va_arg is called repeatedly until this 0 is reached.

12 Finally, va_end is called to restore the runtime stack (which may have been modified by the earlier calls).

The sample call,

```
int n = Menu(
   "Open file",
   "Close file",
   "Revert to saved file",
   "Delete file",
   "Quit application",
   0);
```

Will produce the following output:

1. Open file
2. Close file
3. Revert to saved file
4. Delete file
5. Quit application option?

## COMMAND LINE ARGUMENTS

When a programme is executed under an operating system (such as DOS or UNIX), it can be passed zero or more arguments. These arguments appear after the programme executable name and are separated by blanks.

Because they appear on the same line as where operating system commands are issued, they are called. Command line arguments. As an example, consider a programme named sum which prints out the sum of a set of numbers provided to it as command line arguments. Dialog 4.3 illustrates how two numbers are passed as arguments to sum ($ is the UNIX prompt).

```
$ sum 10.4 12.5
22.9
$
```

Command line arguments are made available to a C++ programme via the main function. There are two ways in which main can be defined:

```
int main (void);
int main (int argc, const char* argv[]);
```

The latter is used when the programme is intended to accept command line arguments. The first parameter, argc, denotes the number of arguments passed to the programme (including the name of the programme itself). The second parameter, argv, is an array of the string constants which represent the arguments. For example, given the command line in Dialog 4.3, we have:

```
argc is       3
argv[0]  is   "sum"
argv[1]  is   "10.4"
argv[2]  is   "12.5"
```

Listing 4.12 illustrates a simple implementation for sum. Strings are converted to real numbers using atof, which is defined in stdlib.h.

## Listing 4.12

```
#include <iostream.h>
#include <stdlib.h>
int main (int argc, const char *argv[])
{
    double sum = 0;
    for (int i = 1; i < argc; ++i)
          sum += atof(argv[i]);
    cout << sum << '\n';
    return 0;
}
```

# 4

# Arrays, Pointers and Classes

## DESCRIPTION

In general, only the array itself has a symbolic name, not its elements. Each element is identified by an index which denotes the position of the element in the array. The number of elements in an array is called its dimension. The dimension of an array is fixed and predetermined; it cannot be changed during programme execution. Arrays are suitable for representing composite data which consist of many similar, individual items. Examples include: a list of names, a table of world citiesand their current temperatures, or the monthly transactions for a bank account.

A pointer is simply the address of an object in memory. Generally, objects can be accessed in two ways: directly by their symbolic name, or indirectly through a pointer. The act of getting to an object via a pointer to it, is called dereferencing the pointer. Pointer variables are defined to point to objects of a specific type so that when the pointer is dereferenced, a typed object is obtained. Pointers are useful for creating dynamic objects during programme execution. Unlike normal (global and local) objects which are allocated storage on the runtime stack, a dynamic object is allocated memory from a different storage area called the heap. Dynamic objects do not obey the normal scope rules. Their scope is explicitly controlled by the programmer.

A reference provides an alternative symbolic name for an object. Accessing an object through a reference is exactly the same as accessing it through its original name. References offer the power of pointers and the convenience of direct access to objects. They are used to support the call-by-reference style of function parameters, especially when large objects are being passed to functions.

## ARRAYS

An array variable is defined by specifying its dimension and the type of its elements. For example, an array representing 10 height measurements (each being an integer quantity) may be defined as:

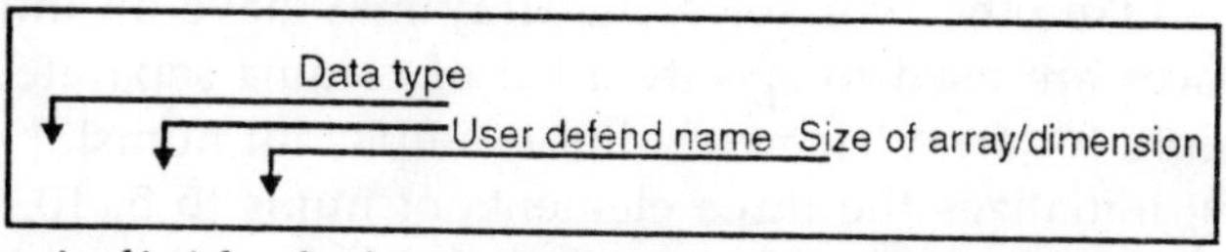


The individual elements of the array are accessed by indexing the array. The first array element always has the index 0. Therefore, heights[0] and heights[9] denote, respectively, the first and last element of heights. Each of heights elements can be treated as an integer variable.

*So, for example, to set the third element to 177, we may write:*

```
heights[2] = 177;
```

Attempting to access a nonexistent array element (*e.g.*, heights[-1] or heights[10]) leads to a serious runtime error (called 'index out of bounds' error). Processing of an array usually involves a loop which goes through the array element by element. Listing 5.13 illustrates this using a function which takes an array of integers and returns the average of its elements.

### Listing

```
#include<iostream.h>
const int size = 3;
void main()
{
    int nums[size];
    cout<<"Enter the element of array";
    for (int register i = 0; i < size; ++i)
    cin>>nums[i];
```

```
    double  Average(int[]);
    cout<<"AVERAGE="<<Average(nums);
}
double Average (int nums[])
{
    double average = 0;
    for (register i = 0; i < size; ++i)
         average += nums[i];
    return average/size;
}
```

Like other variables, an array may have an initialized. Braces are used to specify a list of comma-separated initial values for array elements. For example, int nums[3] = {5, 10, 15}; initializes the three elements of nums to 5, 10, and 15, respectively. When the number of values in the initializer is less than the number of elements, the remaining elements are initialized to zero:

```
int nums[3] = {5, 10};    //nums[2]
   initializes to 0
```

When a complete initializer is used, the array dimension becomes redundant, because the number of elements is implicit in the initializer.

*The first definition of nums can therefore be equivalently written as:*

```
int nums[] = {5, 10, 15}; //no dimension
   needed
```

Another situation in which the dimension can be omitted is for an array function parameter. For example, the Average function above can be improved by rewriting it so that the dimension of nums is not fixed to a constant, but specified by an additional parameter. Listing 5.14 illustrates this.

**Listing**

```
double Average (int nums[], int size)
{
   double average = 0;
for (register i = 0; i < size; ++i)
   average += nums[i];
```

```
return average/size;
}
```

A C++ string is simply an array of characters. For example,

```
char str[] = "HELLO";
```

defines str to be an array of six characters: five letters and a null character. The terminating null character is inserted by the compiler. By contrast,

```
char str[] = {'H', 'E', 'L', 'L', 'O'};
```

defines str to be an array of five characters. It is easy to calculate the dimension of an array using the sizeof operator. For example, given an array ar whose element type is Type, the dimension of ar is:

```
sizeof(ar)/sizeof(Type)
```

## MULTIDIMENSIONAL ARRAYS

An array may have more than one dimension (*i.e.*, two, three, or higher). The organization of the array in memory is still the same (a contiguous sequence of elements), but the programmer's perceived organization of the elements is different. For example, suppose we wish to represent the average seasonal temperature for three major Australian capital cities.

**Table. Average Seasonal Temperature.**

| | Spring | Summer | Autumn | Winter |
|---|---|---|---|---|
| Sydney | 26 | 34 | 22 | 17 |
| Melbourne | 24 | 32 | 19 | 13 |
| Brisbane | 28 | 38 | 25 | 20 |

This may be represented by a two-dimensional array of integers: int seasonTemp. The organization of this array in memory is as 12 consecutive integer elements. The programmer, however, can imagine it as three rows of four integer entries each. The array may be initialized using a nested initializer:

```
int seasonTemp[3][4] =
{
   {26, 34, 22, 17},
```

```
    {24, 32, 19, 13},
    {28, 38, 25, 20}
};
```

Because this is mapped to a one-dimensional array of 12 elements in memory, it is equivalent to:

```
int seasonTemp =
{
    26, 34, 22, 17, 24, 32, 19, 13, 28, 38,
    25, 20
};
```

The nested initializer is preferred because as well as being more informative, it is more versatile. For example, it makes it possible to initialize only the first element of each row and have the rest default to zero:

```
int seasonTemp = {{26}, {24}, {28}};
```

We can also omit the first dimension (but not subsequent dimensions) and let it be derived from the initializer:

```
int seasonTemp =
{
    {26, 34, 22, 17},
    {24, 32, 19, 13},
    {28, 38, 25, 20}
};
```

Processing a multidimensional array is similar to a one-dimensional array, but uses nested loops instead of a single loop. Listing illustrates this by showing a function for finding the highest temperature in seasonTemp.

## Listing

```
#include<iostream.h>
const int rows = 3;
const int columns = 4;
void main()
{
    int HighestTemp (int [][columns]);
    int seasonTemp[rows][columns] = {{26, 34,
    22, 17},
                                  {24, 32, 19, 13},
```

```
                        {28, 38, 25, 20}
                                        };
    cout<<"Highest Temp="<<HighestTemp(seasonTemp);
}
    int HighestTemp (int temp[][columns])
{
    int highest = 0;
    for (register i = 0; i < rows; ++i)
    {
        for (register j = 0; j < columns; ++j)
        {
            if (temp[i][j] > highest)
            {
                highest = temp[i][j];
            }
        }
    }
    return highest;
}
```

*Example*: Programme for multiplication of two matrix

```
#include<iostream.h>
#include<conio.h>
void main()
{
   int a[12][12],b[12][12],c[12][12],i,j,k;
   int row1,column1,row2,column2;;
   clrscr();
   cout<<"Enter rows and columns of 1st matrix: ";
   cin>>row1>>column1;
   cout<<"Enter rows and columns of 2nd matrix: ";
   cin>>row2>>column2;
   if(row1==column2)
   {
   cout<<"Enter the element of 1st Matrix\n";
```

```
    for(i=1;i<=row1;i++)
    {
          for(j=1;j<=column1;j++)
          {
                gotoxy(j*3,i*4+2);
                cin>>a[i][j];
          }
    }
    cout<<"Enter the element of 2nd Matrix\n";
    for(i=1;i<=row2;i++)
    {
          for(j=1;j<=column2;j++)
          {
                gotoxy(j*3,1+i*i+11);
                cin>>b[i][j];
          }
    }
    for(i=1;i<=row1;i++)
    {
          for(j=1;j<=column1;j++)
          {
          c[i][j]=0;
          for(k=1;k<=row1;k++)
          {

    c[i][j]=c[i][j]+(a[i][k]*b[k][j]);
          }
    }
}
cout<<"After Multiplication of Matrices\n";
for(i=1;i<=row1;i++)
{
    for(j=1;j<=column1;j++)
    {
          cout<<c[i][j]<<"\t";
    }
    cout<<endl;
    }
```

```
}
else
   cout<<"Multiplication is not possible";
getch();
}
```

## POINTERS

A pointer is simply the *address* of a memory location and provides an indirect way of accessing data in memory. Pointer variable has the ability to store the address of another variavle. A pointer variable is defined to 'point to' data of a specific type.

*For example*:

```
int *ptr1;      //pointer to an int
char *ptr2;     //pointer to a char
```

The *value* of a pointer variable is the address to which it points. For example, given the definitions

```
int num;
```

we can write:

```
ptr1 = &num;
```

The symbol & is the address operator; it takes a variable as argument and returns the memory address of that variable. The effect of the above assignment is that the address of num is assigned to ptr1. Therefore, we say that ptr1 points to num.

## DYNAMIC MEMORY

In addition to the programme stack (which is used for storing global variables and stack frames for function calls), another memory area, called the heap, is provided. The heap is used for dynamically allocating memory blocks during programme execution. As a result, it is also called dynamic memory. Similarly, the programme stack is also called static memory.

Two operators are used for allocating and deallocating memory blocks on the heap. The new operator takes a type as argument and allocated a memory block for an object of that type. It returns a pointer to the allocated block. For example,

```
int *ptr = new int;
char *str = new char[10];
```

Allocate, respectively, a block for storing a single integer and a block large enough for storing an array of 10 characters. Memory allocated from the heap does not obey the same scope rules as normal variables. For example, in

```
void Foo (void)
{
   char *str = new char[10];
   //...
}
```

When Foo returns, the local variable str is destroyed, but the memory block pointed to by str is *not*. The latter remains allocated until explicitly released by the programmer. The delete operator is used for releasing memory blocks allocated by new. It takes a pointer as argument and releases the memory block to which it points.

*For example*:

```
delete ptr;              //delete an object
delete [] str;           //delete an array of
   objects
```

Note that when the block to be deleted is an array, an additional [] should be included to indicate this.

The significance of this will be explained later when we discuss classes. Should delete be applied to a pointer which points to anything but a dynamically-allocated object (*e.g.*, a variable on the stack), a serious runtime error may occur. It is harmless to apply delete to the 0 pointer. Dynamic objects are useful for creating data which last beyond the function call which creates them. Listing illustrates this using a function which takes a string parameter and returns a *copy* of the string.

## Listing

```
#include <string.h>
char* CopyOf (const char *str)
{
   char *copy = new char[strlen(str) + 1];
   strcpy(copy, str);
   return copy;
}
```

## ANNOTATION

1 This is the standard string header file which declares a variety of functions for manipulating strings.

4 The strlen function (declared in string.h) counts the characters in its string argument up to (but excluding) the final null character. Because the null character is not included in the count, we add 1 to the total and allocate an array of characters of that size.

5 The strcpy function (declared in string.h) copies its second argument to its first, character by character, including the final null character.

Because of the limited memory resources, there is always the possibility that dynamic memory may be exhausted during programme execution, especially when many large blocks are allocated and none released.

Should new be unable to allocate a block of the requested size, it will return 0 instead. It is the responsibility of the programmer to deal with such possibilities. The exception handling mechanism of C++ provides a practical method of dealing with such problems.

## POINTER ARITHMETIC

In C++ one can add an integer quantity to or subtract an integer quantity from a pointer. This is frequently used by programmers and is called pointer arithmetic. Pointer arithmetic is *not* the same as integer arithmetic, because the outcome depends on the size of the object pointed to. For example, suppose that an int is represented by 4 bytes. Now, given,

```
char *str = "HELLO";
int nums[] = {10, 20, 30, 40};
int *ptr = &nums[0];        //pointer to first
   element
```

str++ advances str by one char (*i.e.*, one byte) so that it points to the second character of "HELLO", whereas ptr++ advances ptr by one int (*i.e.*, four bytes) so that it points to the second element of nums. Figure illustrates this diagrammatically.

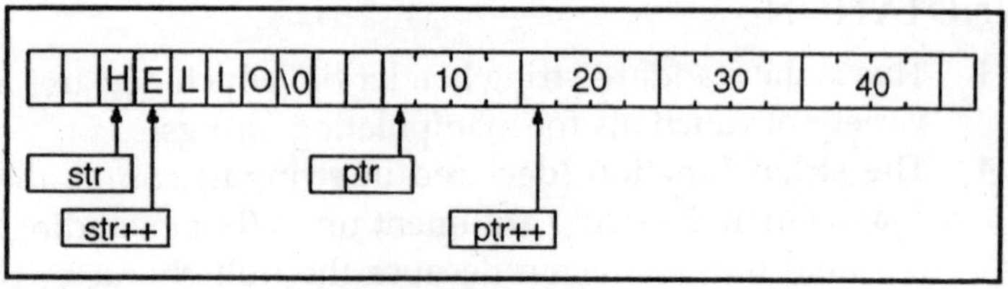


**Fig.** Pointer Arithmetic.

It follows, therefore, that the elements of "HELLO" can be referred to as *str, *(str + 1), *(str + 2), etc. Similarly, the elements of nums can be referred to as *ptr, *(ptr + 1), *(ptr + 2), and *(ptr + 3).

Another form of pointer arithmetic allowed in C++ involves subtracting two pointers of the same type. For example:

```
int *ptr1 = &nums[1];
int *ptr2 = &nums[3];
int n = ptr2 - ptr1;                    //n becomes 2
```

Pointer arithmetic is very handy when processing the elements of an array.

Listing 5.17 shows as an example a string copying function similar to strcpy

## Listing 5.17

```
1  void CopyString (char *dest, char *src)
2  {
3     while (*dest++ = *src++)
4           ;
5  }
```

## Annotation

3 The condition of this loop assigns the contents of src to the contents of dest and then increments both pointers. This condition becomes 0 when the final null character of src is copied to dest.

In turns out that an array variable (such as nums) is itself the address of the first element of the array it represents. Hence the elements of nums can also be referred to using pointer arithmetic on nums, that is, nums[i] is equivalent to *(nums + i). The difference between nums and ptr is that nums is a constant, so it cannot be made to point to anything else, whereas ptr is a variable and can be made to point to any other integer. Listing shows how the Highest Temp function can be improved using pointer arithmetic.

**Listing**

```
int HighestTemp (const int *temp, const int rows, const int columns)
{
    int highest = 0;
    for (register i = 0; i < rows; ++i)
        for (register j = 0; j < columns; ++j)
    if (*(temp + i * columns + j) > highest)
    highest = *(temp + i * columns + j);
    return highest;
}
```

**Annotation**

Instead of passing an array to the function, we pass an int pointer and two additional parameters which specify the dimensions of the array. In this way, the function is not restricted to a specific array size. The expression *(temp + i * columns + j) is equivalent to temp in the previous version of this function. HighestTemp can be simplified even further by treating temp as a onedimensional array of row * column integers.This is shown in Listing.

**Listing**

```
int HighestTemp (const int *temp, const int rows, const int columns)
{
    int highest = 0;
    for (register i = 0; i < rows * columns; ++i)
```

```
        if (*(temp + i) > highest)
            highest = *(temp + i);
    return highest;
}
```

## FUNCTION POINTERS

It is possible to take the address of a function and store it in a function pointer. The pointer can then be used to indirectly call the function.

*For example*:

```
int (*Compare)(const char*, const char*);
```

defines a function pointer named Compare which can hold the address of any function that takes two constant character pointers as arguments and returns an integer. The string comparison library function strcmp, for example, is such.

*Therefore*:

```
Compare = &strcmp;        //Compare points to strcmp function
```

The & operator is not necessary and can be omitted:

```
Compare = strcmp;         //Compare points to strcmp function
```

Alternatively, the pointer can be defined and initialized at once:

```
int (*Compare)(const char*, const char*) = strcmp;
```

When a function address is assigned to a function pointer, the two types must match. The above definition is valid because strcmp has a matching function prototype:

```
int strcmp(const char*, const char*);
```

Given the above definition of Compare, strcmp can be either called directly, or indirectly via Compare. The following three calls are equivalent:

```
strcmp("Tom", "Tim");      //direct call
(*Compare)("Tom", "Tim"); //indirect call
Compare("Tom", "Tim");     //indirect call (abbreviated)
```

A common use of a function pointer is to pass it as an argument to another function; typically because the latter requires different versions of the former in different circumstances. A good example is a binary search function for searching through a sorted array of strings. This function may use a comparison function (such as strcmp) for comparing the search string against the array strings. This might not be appropriate for all cases. For example, strcmp is case-sensitive. If we wanted to do the search in a non-case-sensitive manner then a different comparison function would be needed. As shown in Listing making the comparison function a parameter of the search function, we can make the latter independent of the former.

### Listing

```
1  int BinSearch (char *item, char *table[], int n,
2  int (*Compare)(const char*, const char*))
3  {
4      int bot = 0;
5      int top = n - 1;
6      int mid, cmp;
7      while (bot <= top) {
8      mid = (bot + top)/2;
9      if ((cmp = Compare(item,table[mid])) == 0)
10     return mid;                    //return item index
11     else if (cmp < 0)
12             top = mid - 1;         //restrict search to lower half
13     else
14             bot = mid + 1;         //restrict search to upper half
15     }
16     return -1;                     //not found
17 }
```

### Annotation

1 Binary search is a well-known algorithm for searching through a *sorted* list of items. The search list is denoted

by table which is an array of strings of dimension n. The search item is denoted by item.

2 Compare is the function pointer to be used for comparing item against the array elements.

7 Each time round this loop, the search span is reduced by half. This is repeated until the two ends of the search span (denoted by bot and top) collide, or until a match is found.

9 The item is compared against the middle item of the array.

10 If item matches the middle item, the latter's index is returned.

11 If item is less than the middle item, then the search is restricted to the lower half of the array.

14 If item is greater than the middle item, then the search is restricted to the upper half of the array.

16 Returns -1 to indicate that there was no matching item.

The following example shows how BinSearch may be called with strcmp passed as the comparison function:

```
char *cities[] = {"Boston", "London",
    "Sydney", "Tokyo"};
cout << BinSearch("Sydney", cities, 4, strcmp)
    << '\n';
```

This will output 2 as expected.

## REFERENCES

A reference introduces an alias for an object. The notation for defining references is similar to that of pointers, except that & is used instead of *. For example,

```
double num1 = 3.14;
double &num2 = num1;//num is a reference to
    num1
```

defines num2 as a reference to num1. After this definition num1 and num2 both refer to the same object, as if they were the same variable. It should be emphasized that a reference does not create a copy of an object, but merely a symbolic alias for it. Hence, after

```
num1 = 0.16;
```

both num1 and num2 will denote the value 0.16.

A reference must always be initialized when it is defined: it should be an alias for something. It would be illegal to define a reference and initialize it later.

```
double &num3; //illegal: reference without an initializer
num3 = num1;
```

You can also initialize a reference to a constant. In this case a *copy* of the constant is made (after any necessary type conversion) and the reference is set to refer to the copy.

```
int &n = 1;    //n refers to a copy of 1
```

The reason that n becomes a reference to a copy of 1 rather than 1 itself is safety. Consider what could happen if this were not the case.

```
int &x = 1;
++x;
int y = x + 1;
```

The 1 in the first and the 1 in the third line are likely to be the same object (most compilers do constant optimization and allocate both 1's in the same memory location). So although we expect y to be 3, it could turn out to be 4.

However, by forcing x to be a copy of 1, the compiler guarantees that the object denoted by x will be different from both 1's. The most common use of references is for function parameters. Reference parameters facilitates the pass-by-reference style of arguments, as opposed to the pass-by-value style which we have used so far. To observe the differences, consider the three swap functions in Listing.

**Listing**

```
void Swap1 (int x, int y) //pass-by-value (objects)
{
    int temp = x;
    x = y;
    y = temp;
}
void Swap2 (int *x, int *y)     //pass-by-value (pointers)
```

```
8  {
9      int temp = *x;
10     *x = *y;
11     *y = temp;
12 }
13 void Swap3 (int &x, int &y)     //pass-by-reference
14 {
15     int temp = x;
16     x = y;
17     y = temp;
18 }
```

## Annotation

1. Although Swap1 swaps x and y, this has no effect on the arguments passed to the function, because Swap1 receives a *copy* of the arguments. What happens to the copy does not affect the original.
7. Swap2 overcomes the problem of Swap1 by using pointer parameters instead. By dereferencing the pointers, Swap2 gets to the original values and swaps them.
13. Swap3 overcomes the problem of Swap1 by using reference parameters instead. The parameters become aliases for the arguments passed to the function and therefore swap them as intended.Swap3 has the added advantage that its call syntax is the same as Swap1 andinvolves no addressing or dereferencing. The following main function illustrates the differences:

```
int main (void)
{
    int i = 10, j = 20;
    Swap1(i, j);     cout << i << ", " << j << '\n';
    Swap2(&i, &j);   cout << i << ", " << j << '\n';
    Swap3(i, j);     cout << i << ", " << j << '\n';
}
```

*When run, it will produce the following output:*

```
10, 20
20, 10
10, 20
```

## TYPEDEFS

Typedef is a syntactic facility for introducing symbolic names for data types. Just as a reference defines an alias for an object, a typedef defines an alias for a type. Its main use is to simplify otherwise complicated type declarations as an aid to improved readability. Here are a few examples:

```
typedef char *String;
Typedef char Name[12];
typedef unsigned int uint;
```

The effect of these definitions is that String becomes an alias for char*, Name becomes an alias for an array of 12 chars, and uint becomes an alias for unsigned int. Therefore:

```
String  str;  //is the same as: char *str;
Name    name; //is the same as: char
   name[12];
uint    n;    //is the same as: unsigned int
   n;
```

The complicated declaration of Compare in Listing 5.20 is a good candidate for typedef:

```
typedef int (*Compare)(const char*, const
   char*);
int BinSearch (char *item, char *table[],
   int n, Compare comp)
{
   //...
         if ((cmp = comp(item, table[mid]))
   == 0)
               return mid;
   //...
}
```

The typedef introduces Compare as a new type name for any function with the given prototype. This makes BinSearch's signature arguably simpler.

## CLASSES

A class definition consists of two parts: header and body. The class header specifies the class name and its base classes. The class body defines the class members. Two types of members are supported.

- Data members have the syntax of variable definitions and specify the representation of class objects.
- Member functions have the syntax of function prototypes and specify the class operations, also called the class interface. Class members fall under one of three different access permission categories:
- Public members are accessible by all class users.
- Private members are only accessible by the class members.
- Protected members are only accessible by the class members and the members of a derived class.

The data type defined by a class is used in exactly the same way as a built-in type.

## A SIMPLE CLASS

Listing shows the definition of a simple class for representing points in two dimensions.

### Listing

```
1  class Point {
2     int xVal, yVal;
3  public:
4     void SetPt (int, int);
5     void OffsetPt (int, int);
6  };
```

### Annotation

1 This line contains the class header and names the class as Point. A class definition always begins with the keyword class, followed by the class name. An open brace marks the beginning of the class body.

2 This line defines two data members, xVal and yVal, both of type int. The default access permission for a

class member is private. Both xVal and yVal are therefore private.

3 This keyword specifies that from this point onward the class members are public.

4-5 These two are public member functions. Both have two integer parameters and a void return type.

6 This brace marks the end of the class body.

The order in which the data and member functions of a class are presented is largely irrelevant. The above class, for example, may be equivalently written as:

```
class Point {
public:
   void SetPt (int, int);
   void OffsetPt (int, int);
private:
   int xVal, yVal;
};
```

The actual definition of the member functions is usually not part of the class and appears separately. Listing shows the separate definition of SetPt and OffsetPt.

## Listing

```
1  void Point::SetPt (int x, int y)
2  {
3     xVal = x;
4     yVal = y;
5  }
6  void Point::OffsetPt (int x, int y)
7  {
8     xVal += x;
9     yVal += y;
10 }
```

## Annotation

1 The definition of a class member function is very similar to a normal function. The function name should be preceded by the class name and a double-colon. This identifies SetPt as being a member of Point.

The function interface must match its earlier interface definition within the class (*i.e.*, take two integer parameters and have the return type void).

3-4 Note how SetPt (being a member of Point) is free to refer to xVal and yVal. Non-member functions do not have this privilege.

Once a class is defined in this way, its name denotes a new data type, allowing us to define variables of that type.

*For example*:

```
Point pt; //pt is an object of class Point
pt.SetPt(10,20);     //pt is set to (10,20)
pt.OffsetPt(2,2);    //pt becomes (12,22)
```

Member functions are called using the dot notation: pt.SetPt(10,20) calls SetPt for the object pt, that is, pt is an implicit argument to SetPt.

By making xVal and yVal private members of the class, we have ensured that a user of the class cannot manipulate them directly:

```
pt.xVal = 10;        //illegal
```

This will not compile.

At this stage, we should clearly distinguish between object and class. A class denotes a type, of which there is only one. An object is an element of a particular type (class), of which there may be many. For example,

```
Point pt1, pt2, pt3;
```

defines three objects (pt1, pt2, and pt3) all of the same class (Point). Furthermore, operations of a class are applied to objects of that class, but never the class itself. A class is therefore a concept that has no concrete existence other than that reflected by its objects.

## INLINE MEMBER FUNCTIONS

Inline function is used in c++ for increasing the execution speed of programme. The coding of inline function is same as ordinary user defined function except that inline keyword inserting befor its definition. Inline functions are functions where the call is made to inline functions. The actual code then gets placed in the calling programme. An easier way of defining member functions to be inline is to include their definition *inside* the class.

```
class Point
{
   int xVal, yVal;
public:
   void SetPt (int x,int y) {xVal = x; yVal
   = y;}
   void OffsetPt (int x,int y) {xVal += x;
   yVal += y;}
};
```

Note that because the function body is included, no semicolon is needed after the prototype. Furthermore, all function parameters must be named.

## EXAMPLE: A SET CLASS

A set is an unordered collection of objects with no repetitions. This example shows how a set may be defined as a class. For simplicity, we will restrict ourselves to sets of integers with a finite number of elements. Listing 6.24 shows the Set class definition.

### Listing 6.24

```
#include <iostream.h>
const   maxCard = 100;
enum    Bool {false, true};
class Set {
public:
   void EmptySet   (void)      {card = 0;}
   Bool Member     (const int);
   void AddElem    (const int);
   void RmvElem    (const int);
   void Copy            (Set&);
   Bool Equal      (Set&);
   void Intersect  (Set&, Set&);
   void Union      (Set&, Set&);
   void Print      (void);
private:
```

```
16     int elems[maxCard];       //set elements
17     int card;                 //set cardinality
18 };
```

## Annotation

2 MaxCard denotes the maximum number of elements a set may have.

6 EmptySet clears the contents of the set by setting its cardinality to zero.

7 Member checks if a given number is an element of the set.

8 AddElem adds a new element to the set. If the element is already in the set then nothing happens. Otherwise, it is inserted. Should this result in an overflow then the element is not inserted.

9 RmvElem removes an existing element from the set, provided that element is already in the set.

10 Copy copies one set to another. The parameter of this function is a reference to the destination set.

11 Equal checks if two sets are equal. Two sets are equal if they contain exactly the same elements (the order of which is immaterial).

12 Intersect compares two sets to produce a third set (denoted by its last parameter) whose elements are in both sets. For example, the intersection of {2,5,3} and {7,5,2} is {2,5}.

13 Union compares two sets to produce a third set (denoted by its last parameter) whose elements are in either or both sets. For example, the union of {2,5,3} and {7,5,2} is {2,5,3,7}.

14 Print prints a set using the conventional mathematical notation. For example, a set containing the numbers 5, 2, and 10 is printed as {5,2,10}.

16 The elements of the set are represented by the elems array.

17 The cardinality of the set is denoted by card. Only the first card entries in elems are considered to be valid elements.

The separate definition of the member functions of a class is sometimes referred to as the implementation of the class.

*The implementation of the Set class is as follows:*

```
Bool Set::Member (const int elem)
{
   for (register i = 0; i < card; ++i)
         if (elems[i] == elem)
               return true;
   return false;
}
void Set::AddElem (const int elem)
{
   if (Member(elem))
         return;
   if (card < maxCard)
         elems[card++] = elem;
   else
         cout << "Set overflow\n";
}
void Set::RmvElem (const int elem)
{
   for (register i = 0; i < card; ++i)
         if (elems[i] == elem) {
               for (; i < card-1; ++i)//shift
   elements left
                     elems[i] = elems[i+1];
               —card;
         }
}
void Set::Copy (Set &set)
{
   for (register i = 0; i < card; ++i)
   set.elems[i] = elems[i];
   set.card = card;
}
Bool Set::Equal (Set &set)
{
   if (card != set.card)
         return false;
   for (register i = 0; i < card; ++i)
```

```
    if (!set.Member(elems[i]))
          return false;
    return true;
}
void Set::Intersect (Set &set, Set &res)
{
    res.card = 0;
    for (register i = 0; i < card; ++i)
          if (set.Member(elems[i]))
                res.elems[res.card++] =
    elems[i];
}
void Set::Union (Set &set, Set &res)
{
    set.Copy(res);
    for (register i = 0; i < card; ++i)
          res.AddElem(elems[i]);
}
void Set::Print (void)
{
    cout << "{";
    for (int i = 0; i < card-1; ++i)
          cout << elems[i] << ",";
    if (card > 0)//no comma after the last
    element
          cout << elems[card-1];
    cout << "}\n";
}
```

The following main function creates three Set objects and exercises some of its member functions.

```
int main (void)
{
    Set s1, s2, s3;
    s1.EmptySet(); s2.EmptySet();
    s3.EmptySet();
    s1.AddElem(10);s1.AddElem(20);
    s1.AddElem(30);s1.AddElem(40);
```

```
    s2.AddElem(30); s2.AddElem(50);
    s2.AddElem(10); s2.AddElem(60);
    cout << "s1 = "; s1.Print();
    cout << "s2 = "; s2.Print();
    s2.RmvElem(50);          cout << "s2 - {50}
    = ";          s2.Print();
    if (s1.Member(20))       cout << "20 is in
    s1\n";
    s1.Intersect(s2,s3);     cout << "s1 intsec
    s2 = ";     s3.Print();
    s1.Union(s2,s3);         cout << "s1 union
    s2 = ";     s3.Print();
    if (!s1.Equal(s2))       cout << "s1/=
    s2\n";
    return 0;
}
```

*When run, the programme will produce the following output:*

```
s1 = {10,20,30,40}
s2 = {30,50,10,60}
s2 - {50} = {30,10,60}
20 is in s1
s1 intsec s2 = {10,30}
s1 union s2 = {30,10,60,20,40}
s1/= s2
```

## CONSTRUCTORS

It is possible to define and at the same time initialize objects of a class. This is supported by special member functions called constructors. A constructor always has the same name as the class itself. It never has an explicit return type.It is invoked automatically when the object of that class is created.

## GENERAL SYNTAX OF CONSTRUCTOR

Constructor is a special member function that takes the same name as the class name. The general syntax is as given below:

```
class name(argument1,argument2.......);
```

There are several forms in which a constructor can take its shape namely:

## DEFAULT CONSTRUCTOR

The default constructor takes no parameters. It is also called as no argument constructor.

*For example*:

```
#include<iostream.h>
#include<conio.h>
class integer
{
   int m,n;
   public:
   integer(); //a default constructor
   display()
{
   cout<<"m="<<m;
   cout<<"n="<<n;
}
};
integer::integer()
{
   m=5;
   n=6;
}
void main()
{
   clrscr();
   integer intg(); //a constructor is
   called
   cout<<"output is ";
   intg.display();
   getch();
}
```

## PARAMETRIZED CONSTRUCTOR

Those constructors that accept arguments or parameters are called parametrized constructor. Parmeterized constructor initialize various data elements of different objects with different values when they are created. This objective can be achieved through parameterized constructors.

*For example:*

```
#include <iostream>
class student {
   int a, b;
public:
   student(int i, int j) {
         a=i;
         b=j;
   }
   void show() {
         cout << a << " " << b;
   }
};
int main()
{
   student ob(3, 5);
   ob.show();
}
```

A class may have more than one constructor. To avoid ambiguity, however, each of these must have a unique signature.

*For example:*

```
class Point {
   int xVal, yVal;
public:
   Point (int x, int y)  {xVal = x; yVal =
   y;}
   Point (float, float);        //polar
   coordinates
   Point (void)                 {xVal = yVal = 0;}
         //origin
void OffsetPt (int, int);
};
Point::Point (float len, float angle)
   //polar coordinates
```

```
{
   xVal = (int) (len * cos(angle));
   yVal = (int) (len * sin(angle));
}
```

offers three different constructors. An object of type Point can be defined using any of these:

```
Point pt1(10,20);          //cartesian coordinates
Point pt2(60.3,3.14);      //polar coordinates
Point pt3;                 //origin
```

## COPY CONSTRUCTOR

Copy constructor is used to initialize an object with another object of same class type. Whenever an object is copied, another object is created and in this process the copy constructor gets called. Gernal syntax of copy constructor as follows

User-defined-class-name(User-defined-class-name &temp_object); student(student &obj);

Class name class name pointer to class object student

*For example*:

```
1 Student obj1; //default constructor invocation
2 Student obj2=obj1; // //copy constructor invocation
```

In case of 2nd the compiler will copy the instance obj1 to obj2 member by member. Note that if we are not calling copy constructor explicitly, the default copy constructor is to be executed. Following is the example to create own copy constructor

*Example*:

```
/* Programme to illustrate the concept of
   copy constructor*/
#include<iostream.h>
#include<conio.h>
class student
{
```

```
    private:
          int id,m,n;
    public:
          student()//Default Constructor
          {
          }
          student(int a)//Defination of
    parametrized constructor
          {
                id=a;
          }
          student(student & x)//Defination of
    copy constructor
          {
                id=x.id;
          }
          void display()
          {
                cout<<id;
          }
};
void main()
{
   student a(100);//Parametized constructor
   called
   student b(a);//copy constructor called
   student c=a;//copy constructor called
   clrscr();
   cout<<"\n id of A: ";a.display();
   cout<<"\n id of B: ";b.display();
   cout<<"\n id of C: ";c.display();
   getch();
```

*The following cases may result in a call to a copy constructor:*

1. When an object is returned by value
2. When an object is passed (to a function) by value as an argument
3. When an object is thrown

4. When an object is caught
5. When an object is placed in a brace-enclosed initializer list

## DESTRUCTORS

Just as a constructor is used to initialize an object when it is created, a destructor is used to clean up the object just before it is destroyed. A destructor always has the same name as the class itself, but is preceded with a ~ symbol. Unlike constructors, a class may have at most one destructor. A destructor never takes any arguments and has no explicit return type.

Destructors are generally useful for classes which have pointer data members which point to memory blocks allocated by the class itself. In such cases it is important to release member-allocated memory before the object is destroyed. A destructor can do just that.

For example, our revised version of Set uses a dynamically-allocated array for the elems member. This memory should be released by a destructor:

```
class Set {
public:
        Set (const int size);
        ~Set  (void)  {delete  elems;}//
    destructor
    //...
private:
    int *elems;//set elements
    int maxCard;//maximum cardinality
    int card;//set cardinality
};
```

Now consider what happens when a Set is defined and used in a function:

```
void Foo (void)
{
    Set s(10);
    //...
}
```

When Foo is called, the constructor for s is invoked, allocating storage for s.elems and initializing its data members. Next the rest of the body of Foo is executed. Finally, before Foo returns, the destructor for s is invoked, deleting the storage occupied by s.elems. Hence, as far as storage allocation is concerned, s behaves just like an automatic variable of a built-in type, which is created when its scope is entered and destroyed when its scope is left.

In general, an object's constructor is applied just before the object is *destroyed*. This in turn depends on the object's scope. For example, a global object is destroyed when programme execution is completed; an automatic object is destroyed when its scope is left; and a dynamic object is destroyed when the delete operator is applied to it.

## FRIENDS

Occasionally we may need to grant a function access to the nonpublic members of a class. Such an access is obtained by declaring the function a friend of the class.

*There are two possible reasons for requiring this access*:

1. It may be the only correct way of defining the function.
2. It may be necessary if the function is to be implemented efficiently. overloaded input/output operators. An example of the second case is discussed below.

Suppose that we have defined two variants of the Set class, one for sets of integers and one for sets of reals:

```
class IntSet {
public:
   //...
private:
   int elems[maxCard];
   int card;
};
class RealSet {
public:
   //...
private:
   float elems[maxCard];
```

```
        int card;
    };
```

We want to define a function, SetToReal, which converts an integer set to a real set. We can do this by making the function a member of IntSet:

```
    void IntSet::SetToReal (RealSet &set)
    {
        set.EmptySet();
        for (register i = 0; i < card; ++i)
                set.AddElem((float) elems[i]);
    }
```

Although this works, the overhead of calling AddElem for every member of the set may be unacceptable. The implementation can be improved if we could gain access to the private members of both IntSet and RealSet. This can be arranged by declaring SetToReal as a friend of RealSet.

```
    class RealSet {
        //...
        friend void IntSet::SetToReal (RealSet&);
    };
    void IntSet::SetToReal (RealSet &set)
    {
        set.card = card;
        for (register i = 0; i < card; ++i)
                set.elems[i] = (float) elems[i];
    }
```

The extreme case of having all member functions of a class A as friends of another class B can be expressed in an *abbreviated* form:

```
    class A;
    class B {
        //...
        friend class A;  //abbreviated form
    };
```

Another way of implementing SetToReal is to define it as a global function which is a friend of both classes:

```
    class IntSet {
        //...
```

```
    friend void SetToReal (IntSet&, RealSet&);
};
class RealSet {
    //...
    friend void SetToReal (IntSet&, RealSet&);
};
void SetToReal (IntSet &iSet, RealSet &rSet)
{
    rSet.card = iSet.card;
    for (int i = 0; i < iSet.card; ++i)
          rSet.elems[i]    =    (float)
    iSet.elems[i];
}
```

Although a friend declaration appears inside a class, that does *not* make the function a member of that class. In general, the position of a friend declaration in a class is irrelevant: whether it appears in the private, protected, or the public section, it has the same meaning. Following is the example using friend function.

```
/* Programme to add private member of two
    different classes*/
#include<iostream.h>
#include<conio.h>
class stu;
class student
{
    private:
          int a,b;
    public:
          void getdata();
          friend void sum(student,stu);
};
class stu
{
    public:
          int c,d;
    public:
          void getdata();
```

```
        friend void sum(student,stu);
};
void student::getdata()
{
    cout<<"Enter the a & b";
    cin>>a>>b;
}
void stu::getdata()
{
    cout<<"Enter the c & d";
    cin>>c>>d;
}
void sum(student temp1,stu temp2)
{
    int temp=temp1.a+temp2.c;
    int ab=temp1.b+temp2.d;
    cout<<"temp = "<<temp;
    cout<<"ab = "<<ab;
}
void main()
{
    student obj;
    stu obj1;
    clrscr();
    obj.getdata();
    obj1.getdata();
    sum(obj,obj1);
}
```

## DEFAULT ARGUMENTS

As with global functions, a member function of a class may have default arguments. The same rules apply: all default arguments should be trailing arguments, and the argument should be an expression consisting of objects defined within the scope in which the class appears.

For example, a constructor for the Point class may use default arguments to provide more variations of the way a Point object may be defined:

```
class Point {
   int xVal, yVal;
public:
         Point (int x = 0, int y = 0);
   //...
};
```

Given this constructor, the following definitions are all valid:

```
Point p1;                    //same as: p1(0,
   0)
Point p2(10);          //same as: p2(10, 0)
Point p3(10, 20);
```

Careless use of default arguments can lead to undesirable ambiguity. For example, given the class

```
class Point {
   int xVal, yVal;
public:
         Point (int x = 0, int y = 0);
         Point (float x = 0, float y = 0);/
   /polar coordinates
   //...
};
```

the following definition will be rejected as ambiguous, because it matches both constructors:

```
Point p;         //ambiguous!
```

## IMPLICIT MEMBER ARGUMENT

When a class member function is called, it receives an implicit argument which denotes the particular object (of the class) for which the function is invoked. For example, in

```
Point pt(10,20);
pt.OffsetPt(2,2);
```

pt is an implicit argument to OffsetPt. Within the body of the member function,

one can refer to this implicit argument explicitly as this, which denotes a pointer to the object for which the member is invoked. Using this, OffsetPt can be rewritten as:

```
Point::OffsetPt (int x, int y)
```

```
{
    this->xVal += x; //equivalent to: xVal +=
    x;
    this->yVal += y; //equivalent to: yVal +=
    y;
}
```

Use of this in this particular example is redundant. There are, however, programming cases where the use of the this pointer is essential. We will see examples of such cases in Chapter 7, when discussing overloaded operators.

The this pointer can be used for referring to member functions in exactly the same way as it is used for data members. It is important to bear in mind, however, that this is defined for use within member functions of a class only. In particular, it is undefined for global functions (including global friend functions).

## SCOPE OPERATOR

When calling a member function, we usually use an abbreviated syntax.

*For example*:

```
pt.OffsetPt(2,2);           //abbreviated form
```

This is equivalent to the full form:

```
pt.Point::OffsetPt(2,2); //full form
```

The full form uses the binary scope operator:: to indicate that OffsetPt is a member of Point. In some situations, using the scope operator is essential. For example, the case where the name of a class member is hidden by a local variable (*e.g.*, member function parameter) can be overcome using the scope operator:

```
class Point {
public:
    Point (int x, int y) {Point::x = x;
    Point::y = y;}
    //...
private:
    int x, y;
}
```

Here x and y in the constructor (inner scope) hide x and y in the class (outer scope). The latter are referred to explicitly as Point::x and Point::y.

## MEMBER INITIALIZATION LIST

There are two ways of initializing the data members of a class. The first approach involves initializing the data members using assignments in the body of a constructor. For example:

```
class Image {
public:
        Image (const int w, const int h);
private:
   int width;
   int height;
   //...
};
Image::Image (const int w, const int h)
{
   width = w;
   height = h;
   //...
}
```

The second approach uses a member initialization list in the definition of a constructor.

*For example*:

```
class Image {
public:
        Image (const int w, const int h);
private:
   int width;
   int height;
   //...
};
Image::Image (const int w, const int h):
   width(w), height(h)
{
   //...
}
```

The effect of this declaration is that width is initialized to w and height is initialized to h. The only difference between this approach and the previous one is that here members are initialized *before* the body of the constructor is executed.

A member initialization list may be used for initializing any data member of a class. It is always placed between the constructor header and body.

A colon is used to separate it from the header. It should consist of a comma-separated list of data members whose initial value appears within a pair of brackets.

## CONSTANT MEMBERS

A class data member may defined as constant.

*For example*:

```
class Image {
   const int width;
   const int height;
   //...
};
```

However, data member constants cannot be initialized using the same syntax as for other constants:

```
class Image {
   const int width = 256;        //illegal
   initializer!
   const int height = 168;       //illegal
   initializer!
   //...
};
```

The correct way to initialize a data member constant is through a member initialization list:

```
class Image {
public:
         Image (const int w, const int h);
private:
   const int width;
   const int height;
   //...
};
```

```
Image::Image (const int w, const int h):
   width(w), height(h)
{
   //...
}
```

As one would expect, no member function is allowed to assign to a constant data member.

A constant data member is not appropriate for defining the dimension of an array data member. For example, in

```
class Set {
public:
         Set (void): maxCard(10) {card = 0;}
   //...
private:
   const maxCard;
   int elems[maxCard];    //illegal!
   int card;
};
```

The array elems will be rejected by the compiler for not having a constant dimension. The reason for this being that maxCard is not bound to a value during compilation, but when the programme is run and the constructor is invoked. Member functions may also be defined as constant. This is used to specify which member functions of a class may be invoked for a constant object.

*For example*:

```
class Set {
public:
   Set                  (void)              {card
   = 0;}
   Bool Member          (const int) const;
   void AddElem         (const int);
   //...
};
   Bool Set::Member (const int elem) const
{
   //...
}
```

defines Member as a constant member function. To do so, the keyword const is inserted after the function header, both inside the class and in the function definition. A constant object can only be modified by the constant member functions of the class:

```
const Set s;
s.AddElem(10);//illegal: AddElem not a const
   member
s.Member(10); //ok
```

Given that a constant member function is allowed to be invoked for constant objects, it would be illegal for it to attempt to modify any of the class data members. Constructors and destructors need never be defined as constant members, since they have permission to operate on constant objects.

They are also exempted from the above rule and can assign to a data member of a constant object, unless the data member is itself a constant.

## STATIC MEMBERS

A data member of a class can be defined to be static. This ensures that there will be exactly one copy of the member, shared by all objects of the class. For example, consider a Window class which represents windows on a bitmap display:

```
class Window {
   static Window *first; //linked-list of
   all windows
   Window *next;      //pointer to next window
   //...
};
```

Here, no matter how many objects of type Window are defined, there will be only one instance of first. Like other static variables, a static data member is by default initialized to 0. It can be initialized to an arbitrary value in the same scope where the member function definitions appear:

```
Window *Window::first = &myWindow;
```

The alternative is to make such variables global, but this is exactly what static members are intended to avoid; by including the variable in a class, we can ensure that it will be inaccessible to anything outside the class. Member functions can also be defined to be static. Semantically, a static member function is like a global function which is a friend of the class, but inaccessible outside the class. It does not receive an implicit argument and hence cannot refer to this. Static member functions are useful for defining call-back routines whose parameter lists are predetermined and outside the control of the programmer.

For example, the Window class might use a call-back function for repainting exposed areas of the window:

```
class Window
{
    //...
    static void PaintProc (Event *event);
    //call-back
};
```

Because static members are shared and do not rely on the this pointer, they are best referred to using the *class::member* syntax. For example, first and PaintProc would be referred to as Window::first and Window::PaintProc. Public static members can be referred to using this syntax by nonmember functions.

## MEMBER POINTERS

Recall how a function pointer was used in Chapter 5 to pass the address of a comparison function to a search function. It is possible to obtain and manipulate the address of a member function of a class in a similar fashion. As before, the idea is to make a function more flexible by making it independent of another function. The syntax for defining a pointer to a member function is slightly more complicated, since the class name *must* also be included in the function pointer type. For example, typedef int (Table::*Compare)(const char*, const char*); defines a member function pointer type called Compare for a class called Table. This type will match the address of any member function of Table which takes two constant character pointers and returns an int. Compare may be used for passing a pointer to a Search member of Table:

```
class Table
{
public:
         Table (const int slots);
int      Search (char *item, Compare comp);
int      CaseSesitiveComp (const char*, const
   char*);
int      NormalizedComp (const char*, const
   char*);
private:
int      slots;
char     **entries;
};
```

The definition of Table includes two sample comparison member functions which can be passed to Search.

Search has to use a slightly complicated syntax for invoking the comparison function via comp:

```
int Table::Search (char *item, Compare comp)
{
   int bot = 0;
   int top = slots - 1;
   int mid, cmp;
   while (bot <= top)
{
         mid = (bot + top)/2;
         if ((cmp = (this->*comp)(item,
   entries[mid])) == 0)
               return mid;//return item index
         else if (cmp < 0)
               top = mid - 1;//restrict search
   to lower half
         else
               bot = mid + 1;//restrict search
   to upper half
   }
return -1;//not found
}
```

Note that comp can only be invoked via a Table object (the this pointer is used in this case). None of the following attempts, though seemingly reasonable, will work:

```
(*comp)(item, entries[mid]);   //illegal:
    no class object!
(Table::*comp)(item, entries[mid]);//illegal:
    no class object!
this->*comp(item, entries[mid]);
    //illegal: need brackets!
```

The last attempt will be interpreted as:

```
this->*(comp(item, entries[mid]));//
    unintended precedence!
```

Therefore the brackets around this->*comp are necessary. Using a Table object instead of this will require the following syntax:

```
Table tab(10);
(tab.*comp)(item, entries[mid])
```

Search can be called and passed either of the two comparison member functions of Table.

*For example*:

```
tab.Search("Sydney", Table::NormalizedComp);
```

The address of a data member can be obtained using the same syntax as for a member function.

*For example*:

```
int Table::*n = &Table::slots;
int m = this->*n;
int p = tab.*n;
```

The above class member pointer syntax applies to all members except for static. Static members are essentially global entities whose scope has been limited to a class. Pointers to static members use the conventional syntax of global entities.

In general, the same protection rules apply as before: to take the address of a class member (data or function) one should have access to it. For example, a function which does not have access to the private members of a class cannot take the address of any of those members.

## REFERENCES MEMBERS

A class data member may defined as reference.

*For example:*

```
class Image {
   int width;
   int height;
   int &widthRef;
   //...
};
```

As with data member constants, a data member reference cannot be initialized using the same syntax as for other references:

```
class Image {
   int width;
   int height;
   int &widthRef = width; //illegal!
   //...
};
```

The correct way to initialize a data member reference is through a member
initialization list:

```
class Image
{
public:
        Image (const int w, const int h);
private:
   int width;
   int height;
   int &widthRef;
   //...
};
Image::Image (const int w, const int h):
   widthRef(width)
{
   //...
}
```

This causes widthRef to be a reference for width.

## CLASS OBJECT MEMBERS

A data member of a class may be of a user-defined type,

that is, an object of another class. For example, a Rectangle class may be defined using two Point data members which represent the top-left and bottom-right corners of the rectangle:

```
class Rectangle
{
public:
        Rectangle (int left, int top, int
    right, int bottom);
    //...
private:
    Point topLeft;
    Point botRight;
};
```

The constructor for Rectangle should also initialize the two object members of the class. Assuming that Point has a constructor, this is done by including topLeft and botRight in the member initialization list of the constructor for Rectangle:

```
Rectangle::Rectangle (int left, int top, int
    right, int bottom)
    :                   topLeft(left,top),
    botRight(right,bottom)
{
}
```

If the constructor for Point takes no parameters, or if it has default arguments for all of its parameters, then the above member initialization list may be omitted. Of course, the constructor is still implicitly called.

The order of initialization is always as follows. First, the constructor for topLeft is invoked, followed by the constructor for botRight, and finally the constructor for Rectangle itself. Object destruction always follows the opposite direction.

First the destructor for Rectangle (if any) is invoked, followed by the destructor for botRight, and finally for topLeft. The reason that topLeft is initialized before botRight is not that it appears first in the member initialization list, but because it appears before botRight in the class itself.

Therefore, defining the constructor as follows would *not* change the initialization (or destruction) order:

```
Rectangle::Rectangle (int left, int top, int
   right, int bottom)
   :         botRight(right,bottom),
   topLeft(left,top)
{
}
```

## OBJECT ARRAYS

An array of a user-defined type is defined and used much in the same way as an array of a built-in type. For example, a pentagon can be defined as an array of 5 points:

```
Point pentagon[5];
```

This definition assumes that Point has an 'argument-less' constructor (*i.e.*, one which can be invoked without arguments). The constructor is applied to each element of the array. The array can also be initialized using a normal array initializer. Each entry in the initialization list would invoke the constructor with the desired arguments. When the initializer has less entries than the array dimension, the remaining elements are initialized by the argument-less constructor. For example,

```
Point pentagon[5] =
{
   Point(10,20), Point(10,30), Point(20,30),
   Point(30,20)
};
```

initializes the first four elements of pentagon to explicit points, and the last element is initialized to (0,0). When the constructor can be invoked with a single argument, it is sufficient to just specify the argument.

*For example*:

```
Set sets[4] = {10, 20, 20, 30};
```

is an abbreviated version of:

```
Set sets[4] = {Set(10), Set(20), Set(20),
   Set(30)};
```

An array of objects can also be created dynamically using new:

```
Point *petagon = new Point[5];
```

When the array is finally deleted using delete, a pair of [] should be included:

```
delete [] pentagon; //destroys all array
   elements
```

Unless the [] is included, delete will have no way of knowing that pentagon denotes an array of points and not just a single point. The destructor (if any) is applied to the elements of the array in reverse order before the array is deleted.

Omitting the [] will cause the destructor to be applied to just the first element of the array:

```
delete pentagon;//destroys only the first
   element!
```

Since the objects of a dynamic array cannot be explicitly initialized at the time of creation, the class must have an argument-less constructor to handle the implicit initialization. When this implicit initialization is insufficient, the programmer can explicitly reinitialize any of the elements later:

```
pentagon[0].Point(10, 20);
pentagon[1].Point(10, 30);
//...
```

Dynamic object arrays are useful in circumstances where we cannot predetermine the size of the array. For example, a general polygon class has no way of knowing in advance how many vertices a polygon may have:

```
class Polygon
{
public:
   //...
private:
   Point *vertices;//the vertices
   int nVertices;//the number of vertices
};
```

## CLASS SCOPE

A class introduces a class scope much in the same way a function (or block) introduces a local scope. All the class members belong to the class scope and thus hide entities with identical names in the enclosing scope. For example, in

```
int fork (void);     //system fork
   class Process
{
   int fork (void);
   //...
};
```

the member function fork hides the global system function fork. The former can refer to the latter using the unary scope operator:

```
int Process::fork (void)
{
   int pid =::fork();     //use   global
   system fork
   //...
}
```

*A class itself may be defined at any one of three possible scopes*:

1. *At the global scope*: This leads to a global class, whereby it can be referred to by all other scopes. The great majority of C++ classes (including all the examples presented so far in this chapter) are defined at the global scope.
2. *At the class scope of another class*: This leads to a nested class, where a class is contained by another class.
3. *At the local scope of a block or function*: This leads to a local class, where the class is completely contained by a block or function. A nested class is useful when a class is used only by one other class.

*For example*:

```
class Rectangle {   //a nested class
public:
         Rectangle (int, int, int, int);
   //..
private:
   class Point {
   public:
         Point (int, int);
   private:
         int x, y;
```

```
};
Point topLeft, botRight;
};
```

defines Point as nested by Rectangle. The member functions of Point may be defined either inline inside the Point class or at the global scope.

The latter would require further qualification of the member function names by preceding them with Rectangle::

```
Rectangle::Point::Point (int x, int y)
{
   //...
}
```

A nested class may still be accessed outside its enclosing class by fully qualifying the class name. The following, for example, would be valid at any scope (assuming that Point is made public within Rectangle):

```
Rectangle::Point pt(1,1);
```

A local class is useful when a class is used by only one function — be it a global function or a member function — or even just one block.

*For example*:

```
void Render (Image &image)
{
   class ColourTable {
   public:
         ColourTable(void) {/*... */}
         AddEntry   (int r, int g, int b) {/
   *... */}
         //...
   };
   ColourTable colours;
   //...
}
```

defines ColourTable as a class local to Render.

Unlike a nested class, a local class is not accessible outside the scope within which it is defined. The following, therefore, would be illegal at the global scope:

```
ColourTable ct;     //undefined!
```

A local class must be completely defined inside the scope in which it appears. All of its functions members, therefore, need to be defined inline inside the class. This implies that a local scope is not suitable for defining anything but very simple classes.

## STRUCTURES AND UNIONS

A structure is a class all of whose members are by default public. (Remember that all of the members of a class are by default private.) Structures are defined using the same syntax as classes, except that the keyword struct is used instead of class. For example,

```
struct Point
{
        Point (int, int);
    void OffsetPt (int, int);
    int x, y;
};
```

is equivalent to:

```
class Point
{
public:
        Point (int, int);
    void OffsetPt (int, int);
    int x, y;
};
```

The struct construct originated in C, where it could only contain data members. It has been retained mainly for backward compatibility reasons. In C, a structure can have an initializer with a syntax similar to that of an array. C++ allows such initializers for structures and classes all of whose data members are public:

```
class Employee
{
public:
    char *name;
    int age;
    double salary;
```

```
};
Employee emp = {"Jack", 24, 38952.25};
```

The initializer consists of values which are assigned to the data members of the structure (or class) in the order they appear. This style of initialization is largely superseded by constructors. Furthermore, it cannot be used with a class that has a constructor.

A union is a class all of whose data members are mapped to the same address within its object (rather than sequentially as is the case in a class). The size of an object of a union is, therefore, the size of its largest data member. The main use of unions is for situations where an object may assume values of different types, but only one at a time.

For example, consider an interpreter for a simple programming language, called P, which supports a number of data types such as: integers, reals, strings, and lists. A value in this language may be defined to be of the type:

```
union Value
{
    long integer;
    double real;
    char *string;
    Pair list;
    //...
};
```

where Pair is itself a user-defined type for creating lists:

```
class Pair
{
    Value *head;
    Value *tail;
    //...
};
```

Assuming that a long is 4 bytes, a double 8 bytes, and a pointer 4 bytes, an object of type Value would be exactly 8 bytes, *i.e.*, the same as the size of a double or a Pair object (the latter being equal to two pointers). An object in P can be represented by the class,

```
class Object
```

```
{
private:
    enum ObjType {intObj, realObj, strObj,
    listObj};
    ObjType type;     //object type
    Value val;        //object value
    //...
};
```

where type provides a way of recording what type of value the object currently has. For example, when type is set to strObj, val.string is used for referring to its value.

Because of the unique way in which its data members are mapped to memory, a union may *not* have a static data member or a data member which requires a constructor.

Like a structure, all of the members of a union are by default public. The keywords private, public, and protected may be used inside a struct or a union in exactly the same way they are used inside a class for defining private, public, and protected members.

## BIT FIELDS

It is sometimes desirable to directly control an object at the bit level, so that as many individual data items as possible can be packed into a bit stream without worrying about byte or word boundaries. For example, in data communication, data is transferred in discrete units called packets. In addition to the user data that it carries, each packet also contains a header which is comprised of network-related information for managing the transmission of the packet across the network. To minimize the cost of transmission, it is desirable to minimize the space taken by the header. illustrates how the header fields are packed into adjacent bits to achieve this.

A bit field is referred to in exactly the same way as any other data member. Because a bit field does not necessarily start on a byte boundary, it is illegal to take its address. For the same reason, a bit field cannot be defined as static. Use of enumerations can make working with bit fields easier. For example, given the enumerations

```
enum PacketType      {dataPack, controlPack,
   supervisoryPack};
enum Bool                     {false, true};
```

*we can write*:

```
Packet p;
p.type = controlPack;
p.acknowledge = true;
```

## QUESTIONS

Q1. Explain why the Set parameters of the Set member functions are declared as references.

Q2. Define a class named Complex for representing complex numbers. A complex number has the general form a + *i*b, where a is the real part and b is the imaginary part (*i* stands for imaginary). Complex arithmetic rules are as follows:

```
(a + ib) + (c + id) = (a + c) + i(b + d)
(a + ib) - (c + id) = (a + c) - i(b + d)
(a + ib) * (c + id) = (ac - bd) + i(bc + ad)
```

Define these operations as member functions of Complex.

Q3. Define a class named Menu which uses a linked-list of strings to represent a menu of options. Use a nested class, Option, to represent the set elements. Define a constructor, a destructor, and the following member functions for Menu:

- Insert which inserts a new option at a given position. Provide a default argument so that the item is appended to the end.
- Delete which deletes an existing option.
- Choose which displays the menu and invites the user to choose an option.

Q4. Redefine the Set class as a linked-list so that there would be no restriction on the number of elements a set may have. Use a nested class, Element, to represent the set elements.

Q5. Define a class named Sequence for storing sorted strings. Define a constructor, a destructor, and the following member functions for Sequence:

- Insert which inserts a new string into its sort position.
- Delete which deletes an existing string.
- Find which searches the sequence for a given string and returns true if it finds it, and false otherwise.
- Print which prints the sequence strings.

Q6. Define class named BinTree for storing sorted strings as a binary tree. Define the same set of member functions as for Sequence from the previous exercise.

Q7. Define a member function for BinTree which converts a sequence to a binary tree, as a friend of Sequence. Use this function to define a constructor for BinTree which takes a sequence as argument.

Q8. Add an integer ID data member to the Menu class (Exercise 6.33) so that all menu objects are sequentially numbered, starting from 0. Define an inline member function which returns the ID. How will you keep track of the last allocated ID?

Q9. Modify the Menu class so that an option can itself be a menu, thereby allowing nested menus.

## ANSWERS

1. Declaring Set parameters as references avoids their being copied in a call. Call-byreference
   is generally more efficient than call-by-value when the objects involved are larger than the built-in type objects.

2.
```
class Complex
{
public:
              Complex     (double r = 0,
  double i = 0)
                          {real = r; imag =
  i;}
    Complex Add           (Complex &c);
    Complex Subtract      (Complex &c);
    Complex Multiply      (Complex &c);
    void Print            (void);
private:
      double real;                       //
```

```
real part
        double imag;                              //
imaginary part
};
Complex Complex::Add (Complex &c)
{
        return Complex(real + c.real, imag +
c.imag);
}
Complex Complex::Subtract (Complex &c)
{
        return Complex(real - c.real, imag -
c.imag);
}
Complex Complex::Multiply (Complex &c)
{
        return Complex(   real  *  c.real  -
imag * c.imag,
                          imag  *  c.real  +
real * c.imag);
}
void Complex::Print (void)
{
        cout << real << " + i" << imag <<
'\n';
}
```

3.
```
#include <iostream.h>
#include <string.h>
const int end = -1;     //denotes the end
of the list
class Menu
{
public:
                Menu          void)
{first = 0;}
                ~Menu (void);
void Insert       (const char *str, const
int pos = end);
```

```
void Delete     (const int pos = end);
int      Choose      (void);
private:
     class Option {
     public:
                Option
(const char*);
                ~Option
(void)     {delete name;}
           const char* Name
(void)     {return name;}
           Option*& Next
(void)     {return next;}
private:
     char *name;          //option name
     Option *next;                       //
next option
};
     Option *first;     //first option in
the menu
};
     Menu::Option::Option (const char* str)
{
name = new char [strlen(str) + 1];
strcpy(name, str);
next = 0;
}
Menu::~Menu (void)
{
     Menu::Option *handy, *next;
     for (handy = first; handy != 0; handy
= next) {
           next = handy->Next();
           delete handy;
     }
}
void Menu::Insert (const char *str, const
int pos)
```

```
{
Menu::Option      *option      =      new
Menu::Option(str);
Menu::Option *handy, *prev = 0;
int idx = 0;
//set prev to point to before the insertion
position:
for (handy = first; handy != 0 && idx++ !=
pos; handy = handy-
>Next())
     prev = handy;
if (prev == 0) {         //empty list
option->Next() = first; //first entry
first = option;
} else {                 //insert
     option->Next() = handy;
     prev->Next() = option;
     }
}
void Menu::Delete (const int pos)
{
     Menu::Option *handy, *prev = 0;
     int idx = 0;
     //set prev to point to before the
deletion position:
     for (handy = first;
          handy != 0 && handy->Next() !=
0 && idx++ != pos;
          handy = handy->Next())
          prev = handy;
     if (handy != 0) {
          if (prev == 0)//it's the first
entry
               first = handy->Next();
          else//it's not the first
               prev->Next() = handy-
>Next();
          delete handy;
```

```
        }
}
int Menu::Choose (void)
{
        int n, choice;
        Menu::Option *handy = first;
        do {
                n = 0;
                for (handy = first; handy != 0;
handy = handy->Next())
                        cout << ++n << ". " <<
handy->Name() << '\n';
                cout << "Option? ";
                cin >> choice;
        } while (choice <= 0 || choice > n);
        return choice;
}
```

4.
```
#include <iostream.h>
const int maxCard = 10;
enum Bool {false, true};
class Set {
public:
                Set   (void) {first = 0;}
                ~Set  (void);
int             Card  (void);
Bool Member           (const int) const;
void AddElem          (const int);
void RmvElem          (const int);
void Copy  (Set&);
Bool Equal (Set&);
void Intersect  (Set&, Set&);
void Union (Set&, Set&);
void Print (void);
private:
        class Element {
        public:
                Element      (const int val)
{value = val; next = 0;}
```

```
        int   Value (void) {return value;}
        Element*&  Next   (void)
    {return next;}
        private:
             int value;                         //
    element value
             Element *next;                     //
    next element
        };
        Element *first;                         //
    first element in the list
    };
    Set::~Set (void)
    {
        Set::Element *handy, *next;
        for (handy = first; handy != 0; handy
    = next) {
             next = handy->Next();
             delete handy;
        }
    }
    int Set::Card (void)
    {
        Set::Element *handy;
        int card = 0;
        for (handy = first; handy != 0; handy
    = handy->Next())
        ++card;
        return card;
    }
    Bool Set::Member (const int elem) const
    {
        Set::Element *handy;
        for (handy = first; handy != 0; handy
    = handy->Next())
             if (handy->Value() == elem)
                  return true;
        return false;
```

```
}
void Set::AddElem (const int elem)
{
     if (!Member(elem)) {
          Set::Element *option = new
Set::Element(elem);
          option->Next() = first;     //
prepend
          first = option;
     }
}
void Set::RmvElem (const int elem)
{
     Set::Element *handy, *prev = 0;
     int idx = 0;
     //set prev to point to before the
deletion position:
     for (handy = first;
          handy != 0 && handy->Next() !=
0 && handy->Value() != elem;
          handy = handy->Next())
          prev = handy;
     if (handy != 0) {
          if (prev == 0)
//it's the first entry
               first = handy->Next();
          else
     //it's not the first
               prev->Next() = handy-
>Next();
          delete handy;
     }
}
void Set::Copy (Set &set)
{
     Set::Element *handy;
     for (handy = first; handy != 0; handy
= handy->Next())
```

```
            set.AddElem(handy->Value());
}
Bool Set::Equal (Set &set)
{
      Set::Element *handy;
      if (Card() != set.Card())
            return false;
for (handy = first; handy != 0; handy =
handy->Next())
      if (!set.Member(handy->Value()))
            return false;
      return true;
}
void Set::Intersect (Set &set, Set &res)
{
Set::Element *handy;
for (handy = first; handy != 0; handy =
handy->Next())
      if (set.Member(handy->Value()))
            res.AddElem(handy->Value());
}
void Set::Union (Set &set, Set &res)
{
      Copy(res);
      set.Copy(res);
}
void Set::Print (void)
{
      Set::Element *handy;
      cout << '{';
      for (handy = first; handy != 0; handy
= handy->Next()) {
            cout << handy->Value();
            if (handy->Next() != 0)
                  cout << ',';
      }
      cout << "}\n";
}
```

5.
```
#include <iostream.h>
#include <string.h>
enum Bool {false, true};
typedef char *String;
class BinNode;
class BinTree;
class Sequence {
public:
Sequence   (const int size);
~Sequence  (void)      {delete entries;}
void Insert     (const char*);
void Delete     (const char*);
Bool Find       (const char*);
void Print (void);
int        Size         (void)
{return used;}
friend BinNode* BinTree::MakeTree (Sequence
&seq, int low, int high);
protected:
char **entries; //sorted array of string
entries
const int slots;      //number     of
sequence slots
int used;             //number of slots
used so far
};
void
Sequence::Insert (const char *str)
{
      if (used >= slots)
           return;
      for (register i = 0; i < used; ++i) {
           if (strcmp(str,entries[i]) < 0)
           break;
      }
      for (register j = used; j > i; —j)
           entries[j] = entries[j-1];
      entries[i] = new char[strlen(str) +
```

```
1];
        strcpy(entries[i], str);
        ++used;
}
void
Sequence::Delete (const char *str)
{
        for (register i = 0; i < used; ++i) {
                if (strcmp(str,entries[i]) == 0)
{
                        delete entries[i];
                        for (register j = i; j <
used-1; ++j)
                                entries[j]      =
entries[j+1];
                        —used;
                        break;
                }
        }
}
Bool
Sequence::Find (const char *str)
{
        for (register i = 0; i < used; ++i)
                if (strcmp(str,entries[i]) == 0)
                        return true;
        return false;
}
void
Sequence::Print (void)
{
        cout << '[';
        for (register i = 0; i < used; ++i) {
                cout << entries[i];
                if (i < used-1)
                        cout << ',';
        }
cout << "]\n";
```

```
}
```

6.
```
#include <iostream.h>
#include <string.h>
enum Bool {false,true};
class BinNode {
public:
                    BinNode
(const char*);
                    ~BinNode
(void)      {delete value;}
char*&              Value
(void)      {return value;}
BinNode*&           Left
(void)      {return left;}
BinNode*&           Right
(void)      {return right;}
void        FreeSubtree ( B i n N o d e
*subtree);
void        InsertNode  (BinNode *node,
BinNode *&subtree);
void        DeleteNode  (const  char*,
BinNode *&subtree);
const BinNode*  FindNode
(const char*, const BinNode *subtree);
void        PrintNode   (const BinNode
*node);
private:
      char *value;        //node value
      BinNode    *left; //pointer to left
child
      BinNode    *right;//pointer to right
child
};
class BinTree {
public:
            BinTree     (void)
{root = 0;}
            BinTree     (Sequence &seq);
```

```
          ~BinTree    (void)
{root->FreeSubtree(root);}
     void Insert       (const char *str);
     void Delete       (const char *str)
{root->DeleteNode(str, root);}
     Bool Find  (const char *str)
{return root->FindNode(str, root)
                       != 0;}
     void Print(void) { r o o t -
>PrintNode(root); cout << '\n';}
protected:
     BinNode* root;                    //
root node of the tree
}
BinNode::BinNode (const char *str)
{
     value = new char[strlen(str) + 1];
     strcpy(value, str);
     left = right = 0;
}
void
BinNode::FreeSubtree (BinNode *node)
{
     if (node != 0) {
          FreeSubtree(node->left);
          FreeSubtree(node->right);
          delete node;
     }
}
void
BinNode::InsertNode (BinNode *node, BinNode
*&subtree)
{
if (subtree == 0)
     subtree = node;
else if (strcmp(node->value, subtree->value)
<= 0)
     InsertNode(node, subtree->left);
```

```
else
     InsertNode(node, subtree->right);
}
void
BinNode::DeleteNode (const char *str,
BinNode *&subtree)
{
     int cmp;
     if (subtree == 0)
          return;
     if ((cmp = strcmp(str, subtree-
>value)) < 0)
          DeleteNode(str, subtree->left);
     else if (cmp > 0)
          DeleteNode(str, subtree->right);
     else {
          BinNode* handy = subtree;
          if (subtree->left == 0)     //
no left subtree
               subtree = subtree->right;
          else if (subtree->right == 0)
//no right subtree
               subtree = subtree->left;
          else
          {    //left and right subtree
               subtree = subtree->right;
               //insert left subtree into
right subtree:
               InsertNode(subtree->left,
subtree->right);
          }
          delete handy;
     }
}
const BinNode*
BinNode::FindNode (const char *str, const
BinNode *subtree)
{
```

```
        int cmp;
        return (subtree == 0)
                ? 0
: ((cmp = strcmp(str, subtree->value)) < 0
        ? FindNode(str, subtree->left)
                : (cmp > 0
        ? FindNode(str, subtree->right)
                : subtree));
}
void
BinNode::PrintNode (const BinNode *node)
{
        if (node != 0)
        {
                PrintNode(node->left);
                cout << node->value << ' ';
                PrintNode(node->right);
        }
}
BinTree::BinTree (Sequence &seq)
{
        root = MakeTree(seq, 0, seq.Size() -
1);
}
void
BinTree::Insert (const char *str)
{
        root->InsertNode(new BinNode(str),
root);
}
```

7.

```
class Sequence {
        //...
friend BinNode* BinTree::MakeTree (Sequence
&seq, int low, int high);
};
class BinTree {
public:
        //...
```

```
            BinTree (Sequence &seq);
        //...
    BinNode* MakeTree (Sequence &seq, int low,
    int high);
    };
    BinTree::BinTree (Sequence &seq)
    {
        root = MakeTree(seq, 0, seq.Size() -
    1);
    }
    BinNode*
    BinTree::MakeTree (Sequence &seq, int low,
    int high)
    {
        int mid = (low + high)/2;
        BinNode*    node    =    new
    BinNode(seq.entries[mid]);
        node->Left() = (mid == low ? 0:
    MakeTree(seq, low, mid-1));
        node->Right() = (mid == high ? 0:
    MakeTree(seq, mid+1, high));
        return node;
    }
```

8. A static data member is used to keep track of the last allocated ID (see lastId below).

```
class Menu {
public:
    //...
    int ID (void) {return id;}
private:
    //...
    int id;                  //menu ID
    static int lastId;       //last allocated
    ID
};
int Menu::lastId = 0;
```

9.
```
#include <iostream.h>
#include <string.h>
```

```
const int end = -1;     //denotes the end
of the list
class Option;
class Menu {
public:
      Menu  (void)          {first = 0; id =
lastId++;}
      ~Menu (void);
      void  Insert          (const char *str,
const Menu *submenu, const int
pos = end);
      void  Delete          (const int pos =
end);
      int   Print (void);
      int   Choose          (void) const;
      int ID      (void) {return id;}
private:
      class Option {
      public:
                  Option (const char*, const
Menu* = 0);
                  ~Option(void);
      const char*Name
(void)      {return name;}
      const Menu*Submenu(void)
{return submenu;}
      Option*&            Next
(void)      {return next;}
      void        Print  (void);
      int         Choose (void)
const;
private:
      char        *name;                  //
option name
      const Menu  *submenu;
//submenu
      Option              *next;
```

```
//next option
};
Option *first;
//first option in the menu
     int        id;
//menu ID
static int lastId;
//last allocated ID
};
Menu::Option::Option (const char *str, const
Menu *menu):
submenu(menu)
{
     name = new char [strlen(str) + 1];
     strcpy(name, str);
     next = 0;
}
Menu::Option::~Option (void)
{
     delete name;
     delete submenu;
}
void Menu::Option::Print (void)
{
     cout << name;
     if (submenu != 0)
     cout << " ->";
     cout << '\n';
}
int Menu::Option::Choose (void) const
{
     if (submenu == 0)
          return 0;
     else
          return submenu->Choose();
}
int Menu::lastId = 0;
Menu::~Menu (void)
```

```
{
Menu::Option *handy, *next;
     for (handy = first; handy != 0; handy
= next) {
          next = handy->Next();
          delete handy;
     }
}
void Menu::Insert (const char *str, const
Menu *submenu, const int pos)
{
     Menu::Option *option = new Option(str,
submenu);
     Menu::Option *handy, *prev = 0;
     int idx = 0;
     //set prev to point to before the
insertion position:
     for (handy = first; handy != 0 &&
idx++ != pos; handy = handy-
>Next())
          prev = handy;
     if (prev == 0) {
     //empty list
          option->Next() = first;
//first entry
          first = option;
     } else {//insert
          option->Next() = handy;
          prev->Next() = option;
     }
}
void Menu::Delete (const int pos)
{
     Menu::Option *handy, *prev = 0;
     int idx = 0;
     //set prev to point to before the
deletion position:
```

```
	for (handy = first;
		handy != 0 && handy->Next() !=
0 && idx++ != pos;
		handy = handy->Next())
		prev = handy;
	if (handy != 0) {
		if (prev == 0)			//
it's the first entry
			first = handy->Next();
		else//it's not the first
			prev->Next() = handy-
>Next();
		delete handy;
		}
	}
int Menu::Print (void)
{
	int n = 0;
	Menu::Option *handy = first;
	for (handy = first; handy != 0; handy
= handy->Next()) {
		cout << ++n << ". ";
		handy->Print();
	}
return n;
}
int Menu::Choose (void) const
{
	int choice, n;
	do {
		n = Print();
		cout << "Option? ";
		cin >> choice;
	} while (choice <= 0 || choice > n);
	Menu::Option *handy = first;
	n = 1;
	//move to the chosen option:
```

```
      for (handy = first; n != choice &&
handy != 0; handy = handy-
>Next())
            ++n;
      //choose the option:
      n = handy->Choose();
      return (n == 0 ? choice: n);
}
```

# 5

# Overloading

## FUNCTIONAL OVERLOADING

Consider a function, GetTime, which returns in its parameter(s) the current time of the day, and suppose that we require two variants of this function: one which returns the time as seconds from midnight, and one which returns the time as hours, minutes, and seconds. Given that these two functions serve the same purpose, there is no reason for them to have different names.

C++ allows functions to be overloaded, that is, the same function to have more than one definition:

```
long GetTime (void);//seconds from midnight
void GetTime (int &hours, int &minutes, int
    &seconds);
```

When GetTime is called, the compiler compares the number and type of arguments in the call against the definitions of GetTime and chooses the one that matches the call. For example:

```
int h, m, s;
long t = GetTime(); //matches GetTime(void)
GetTime(h, m, s);   //matches GetTime(int&,
    int&, int&);
```

To avoid ambiguity, each definition of an overloaded function must have a unique signature. Member functions of a class may also be overloaded:

```
class Time
{
    //...
```

```
    long GetTime (void);    //seconds   from
    midnight
    void GetTime (int &hours, int &minutes,
    int &seconds);
};
```

Function overloading is useful for obtaining flavours that are not possible using default arguments alone. Overloaded functions may also have default arguments:

```
void Error (int errCode, char *errMsg = "");
void Error (char *errMsg);
```

## OPERATOR OVERLOADING

C++ allows the programmer to define additional meanings for its predefined operators by overloading them. For example, we can overload the + and – operators for adding and subtracting Point objects:

```
class Point
{
public:
    Point (int x,  int y)  {Point::x  =  x;
    Point::y = y;}
    Point operator + (Point &p) {return Point(x
    + p.x,y + p.y);}
    Point operator - (Point &p) {return Point(x
    - p.x,y - p.y);}
private:
    int x, y;
};
```

After this definition, + and - can be used for adding and subtracting points, much in the same way as they are used for adding and subtracting numbers:

```
Point p1(10,20), p2(10,20);
Point p3 = p1 + p2;
Point p4 = p1 - p2;
```

The above overloading of + and - uses member functions. Alternatively, an operator may be overloaded globally:

```
class Point {
public:
```

```
    Point (int x, int y)        {Point::x = x;
    Point::y = y;}
    friend Point operator + (Point    &p,
    Point &q)
                                { r e t u r n
    Point(p.x + q.x,p.y + q.y);}
    friend Point operator -  (Point    &p,
    Point &q)
                                { r e t u r n
    Point(p.x - q.x,p.y - q.y);}
  private:
    int x, y;
};
```

The use of an overloaded operator is equivalent to an explicit call to the function which implements it.

*For example*:

```
operator+(p1, p2)   //is equivalent to: p1
    + p2
```

In general, to overload a predefined operator λ, we define a function named operatorλ.

*If λ is a binary operator*:

- Operator l must take exactly one argument if defined as a class member, or two arguments if defined globally. However, if λ is a unary operator:
- Operator l must take no arguments if defined as a member function, or one argument if defined globally.

Table summarizes the C++ operators which can be overloaded. The remaining five operators cannot be overloaded:

```
.   .*    ::    ?:    sizeof      / / n o t
    overloadable
```

**Table7.10 . Overloadable Operators.**

| Unary: | + | – | * | ! | ~ | & | ++ | – |
|---|---|---|---|---|---|---|---|---|
| () | -> | – | | | | | | |
| | | | | >* | | | | |
| | new | delete | | | | | | |
| Binary: | + | - | * | / | % | & | \| | ^ |

<table>
<tr><td><<</td><td>>></td><td></td><td></td><td></td><td></td><td></td><td></td><td></td></tr>
<tr><td></td><td>=</td><td>+=</td><td>-=</td><td>/=</td><td>%=</td><td>&=</td><td>|=</td><td>^=</td></tr>
<tr><td><<</td><td>>></td><td></td><td></td><td></td><td></td><td></td><td></td><td></td></tr>
<tr><td>=</td><td>=</td><td></td><td></td><td></td><td></td><td></td><td></td><td></td></tr>
<tr><td></td><td>==</td><td>!=</td><td><</td><td>></td><td><=</td><td>>=</td><td>&&</td><td>||</td></tr>
<tr><td>[]</td><td>()</td><td>,</td><td></td><td></td><td></td><td></td><td></td><td></td></tr>
</table>

A strictly unary operator (*e.g.*, ~) cannot be overloaded as binary, nor can a strictly binary operator (*e.g.*, =) be overloaded as unary.

C++ does not support the definition of new operator tokens, because this can lead to ambiguity. Furthermore, the precedence rules for the predefined operators is fixed and cannot be altered. For example, no matter how you overload *, it will always have a higher precedence than +.

Operators ++ and -- can be overloaded as prefix as well as postfix.

Equivalence rules do not hold for overloaded operators. For example, overloading + does not affect + =, unless the latter is also explicitly overloaded. Operators ->, =, [], and () can only be overloaded as member functions, and not globally.

To avoid the copying of large objects when passing them to an overloaded operator, references should be used. Pointers are not suitable for this purpose because an overloaded operator cannot operate exclusively on pointers.

## EXAMPLE: SET OPERATORS

The Set class was introduced in Chapter 6. Most of the Set member functions are better defined as overloaded operators. Listing 7.25 illustrates.

### Listing 7.25

```
#include <iostream.h>
const   maxCard = 100;
enum    Bool {false, true};
class Set {
public:
                 Set          (void)       {card
```

```
    = 0;}
    friend Bool operator & (const int,
    Set&);//membership
    friend Bool operator == (Set&, Set&);
    //equality
    friend Bool operator != (Set&, Set&);
    //inequality
    friend Set operator * (Set&, Set&);
    //intersection
    friend Set operator + (Set&, Set&);
    //union
    //...
    void AddElem (const int elem);
    void Copy (Set &set);
    void Print (void);
private:
    int elems[maxCard];//set elements
    int card;//set cardinality
};
```

Here, we have decided to define the operator functions as global friends. They could have just as easily been defined as member functions. The implementation of these functions is as follow.

```
Bool operator & (const int elem, Set &set)
{
   for (register i = 0; i < set.card; ++i)
         if (elem == set.elems[i])
               return true;
   return false;
}
Bool operator == (Set &set1, Set &set2)
{
   if (set1.card != set2.card)
               return false;
   for (register i = 0; i < set1.card; ++i)
         if (!(set1.elems[i] & set2))
   //use overloaded &
               return false;
```

```
    return true;
}
Bool operator != (Set &set1, Set &set2)
{
    return !(set1 == set2);//use overloaded
    ==
}
Set operator * (Set &set1, Set &set2)
{
    Set res;
    for (register i = 0; i < set1.card; ++i)
          if (set1.elems[i] & set2)//use
    overloaded &
                res.elems[res.card++] =
    set1.elems[i];
    return res;
}
Set operator + (Set &set1, Set &set2)
{
    Set res;
    set1.Copy(res);
    for (register i = 0; i < set2.card; ++i)
          res.AddElem(set2.elems[i]);
    return res;
}
```

The syntax for using these operators is arguably neater than those of the functions they replace, as illustrated by the following main function:

```
int main (void)
{
    Set s1, s2, s3;
    s1.AddElem(10);   s1.AddElem(20);
    s1.AddElem(30); s1.AddElem(40);
    s2.AddElem(30);   s2.AddElem(50);
    s2.AddElem(10); s2.AddElem(60);
    cout << "s1 = "; s1.Print();
    cout << "s2 = "; s2.Print();
    if (20 & s1) cout << "20 is in s1\n";
```

```
    cout << "s1 intsec s2 = "; (s1 *
    s2).Print();
    cout << "s1 union s2 = "; (s1 + s2).Print();
    if (s1 != s2) cout << "s1/= s2\n";
    return 0;
}
```

When run, the programme will produce the following output:

```
s1 = {10,20,30,40}
s2 = {30,50,10,60}
20 is in s1
s1 intsec s2 = {10,30}
s1 union s2 = {10,20,30,40,50,60}
s1/= s2
```

## TYPE CONVERSION

The normal built-in type conversion rules of the language also apply to overloaded functions and operators. For example, in,

```
if ('a' & set)
    //...
```

the first operand of & (*i.e.*, 'a') is implicitly converted from char to int, because overloaded and expects its first operand to be of type int.

Any other type conversion required in addition to these must be explicitly defined by the programmer. For example, suppose we want to overload + for the Point type so that it can be used to add two points, or to add an integer value to both coordinates of a point:

```
class Point {
    //...
    friend Point operator + (Point, Point);
    friend Point operator + (int, Point);
    friend Point operator + (Point, int);
};
```

To make + commutative, we have defined two functions for adding an integer to a point: one for when the integer is the first operand, and one for when the integer is the second operand. It should be obvious that if we start considering other types in addition to int, this approach will ultimately lead to an unmanageable variations of the operator.A better approach is to use a constructor to convert the object to the same type as the class itself so that one overloaded operator can handle the job. In this case, we need a constructor which takes an int, specifying both coordinates of a point:

```
class Point {
    //...
    Point (int x)              {Point::x      =
    Point::y = x;}
    friend Point operator + (Point, Point);
};
```

For constructors of one argument, one need not explicitly call the constructor:

```
Point p = 10;          //equivalent to: Point
    p(10);
```

Hence, it is possible to write expressions that involve variables or constants of type Point and int using the + operator.

```
Point p(10,20), q = 0;
q = p + 5;                    //equivalent to: q
    = p + Point(5);
```

Here, 5 is first converted to a temporary Point object and then added to p. The temporary object is then destroyed. The overall effect is an *implicit* type conversion from int to Point. The final value of q is therefore (15,25).

What if we want to do the opposite conversion, from the class type to another type? In this case, constructors cannot be used because they always return an object of the class to which they belong. Instead, one can define a member function which explicitly converts the object to the desired type.

For example, given a Rectangle class, we can define a type conversion function which converts a rectangle to a point, by overloading the type operator Point in Rectangle:

```
class Rectangle {
public:
    Rectangle (int left, int top, int right,
```

```
    int bottom);
    Rectangle (Point &p, Point &q);
    //...
    operator Point () {return botRight -
    topLeft;}
  private:
    Point topLeft;
    Point botRight;
  };
```

This operator is defined to convert a rectangle to a point, whose coordinates represent the width and height of the rectangle. Therefore, in the code fragment,

```
  Point          p(5,5);
  Rectangle      r(10,10,20,30);
  r + p;
```

rectangle r is first *implicitly* converted to a Point object by the type conversion operator, and then added to p. The type conversion Point can also be applied *explicitly* using the normal type cast notation.

*For example*:

```
 Point(r);//explicit type-cast to a Point
 (Point)r;//explicit type-cast to a Point
```

In general, given a user-defined type X and another (built-in or user-defined)

*type Y*:

- A constructor defined for X which takes a single argument of type Y will implicitly convert Y objects to X objects when needed.
- Overloading the type operator Y in X will implicitly convert X objects to Y objects when needed.

```
  class X
  {
    //...
    X (Y&);//convert Y to X
    operator Y ();//convert X to Y
  };
```

One of the disadvantages of user-defined type conversion methods is that, unless they are used sparingly, they can lead to programmes whose behaviours can be very difficult to predict. There is also the additional risk of creating ambiguity.

Ambiguity occurs when the compiler has more than one option open to it for applying user-defined type conversion rules, and therefore unable to choose. All such cases are reported as errors by the compiler. To illustrate possible ambiguities that can occur, suppose that we also define a type conversion constructor for Rectangle (which takes a Point argument) as well as overloading the + and – operators:

```
class Rectangle {
public:
   Rectangle (int left, int top, int right,
   int bottom);
   Rectangle (Point &p, Point &q);
   Rectangle (Point &p);
   operator Point () {return botRight -
   topLeft;}
   friend Rectangle operator + (Rectangle
   &r, Rectangle &t);
   friend Rectangle operator - (Rectangle
   &r, Rectangle &t);
private:
   Point topLeft;
   Point botRight;
};
```

Now, in

```
Point        p(5,5);
Rectangle    r(10,10,20,30);
r + p;
```

r + p can be interpreted in two ways. Either as

```
r + Rectangle(p)     //yields a Rectangle
```

or as:

```
Point(r) + p              //yields a Point
```

Unless the programmer resolves the ambiguity by explicit type conversion, this will be rejected by the compiler.

## EXAMPLE: BINARY NUMBER CLASS

Listing 7.26 defines a class for representing 16-bit binary numbers as sequences of 0 and 1 characters.

### Listing 7.26

```
1  #include <iostream.h>
2  #include <string.h>
3  int const binSize = 16;
4  class Binary {
5  public:
6     Binary      (const char*);
7     Binary      (unsigned int);
8  friend Binary operator + (const Binary, const Binary);
9                 operator int ();      // type conversion
10          void Print       (void);
11 private:
12          char bits[binSize];         // binary quantity
13 };
```

### Annotation

6 This constructor produces a binary number from its bit pattern.

7 This constructor converts a positive integer to its equivalent binary representation.

8 The + operator is overloaded for adding two binary numbers. Addition is done bit by bit. For simplicity, no attempt is made to detect overflows.

9 This type conversion operator is used to convert a Binary object to an int object.

10 This function simply prints the bit pattern of a binary number.

12 This array is used to hold the 0 and 1 bits of the 16-bit quantity as characters. The implementation of these functions is as follows:

```
Binary::Binary (const char *num)
{
   int iSrc = strlen(num) - 1;
   int iDest = binSize - 1;
   while (iSrc >= 0 && iDest >= 0)    /    /
   copy bits
         bits[iDest–] = (num[iSrc–] == '0' ?
   '0': '1');
while (iDest >= 0)                   //pad
   left with zeros
         bits[iDest–] = '0';
}
Binary::Binary (unsigned int num)
{
   for (register i = binSize - 1; i >= 0; –
   i) {
         bits[i] = (num % 2 == 0 ? '0': '1');
         num >>= 1;
   }
}
Binary operator + (const Binary n1, const
   Binary n2)
{
   unsigned carry = 0;
   unsigned value;
   Binary res = "0";
   for (register i = binSize - 1; i >= 0; –
   i) {
         value = (n1.bits[i] == '0' ? 0: 1)
   +
               (n2.bits[i] == '0' ? 0: 1)
   + carry;
         res.bits[i] = (value % 2 == 0 ?
   '0': '1');
         carry = value >> 1;
   }
   return res;
}
```

```
Binary::operator int ()
{
   unsigned value = 0;
   for (register i = 0; i < binSize; ++i)
         value = (value << 1) + (bits[i] ==
   '0' ? 0: 1);
   return value;
}
void Binary::Print (void)
{
   char str[binSize + 1];
   strncpy(str, bits, binSize);
   str[binSize] = '\0';
   cout << str << '\n';
}
```

The following main function creates two objects of type Binary and tests the + operator.

```
main ()
{
   Binary n1 = "01011";
   Binary n2 = "11010";
   n1.Print();
   n2.Print();
   (n1 + n2).Print();
   cout << n1 + Binary(5) << '\n';    //add
   and then convert to
int
   cout << n1 - 5 << '\n';           /   /
   convert n2 to int and then
subtract
}
```

The last two lines of main behave completely differently. The first of these converts 5 to Binary, does the addition, and then converts the Binary result to int, before sending it to cout.

*This is equivalent to*:

```
cout << (int) Binary::operator+(n2,Binary(5))
   << '\n';
```

The second converts n1 to int (because - is not defined for Binary), performs the subtraction, and then send the result to cout. This is equivalent to:

```
cout << ((int) n2) - 5 << '\n';
```

In either case, the user-defined type conversion operator is applied implicitly. The output produced by the programme is evidence that the conversions are performed correctly:

```
0000000000001011
0000000000011010
0000000000100101
16
6
```

## OVERLOADING << FOR OUTPUT

The simple and uniform treatment of output for built-in types is easily extended to user-defined types by further overloading the << operator. For any given userdefined type T, we can define an operator<< function which outputs objects of type T:

```
ostream& operator << (ostream&, T&);
```

The first parameter must be a reference to ostream so that multiple uses of << can be concatenated. The second parameter need not be a reference, but this is more efficient for large objects. For example, instead of the Binary class's Print member function, we can overload the << operator for the class. Because the first operand of << must be an ostream object, it cannot be overloaded as a member function. It should therefore be defined as a global function:

```
class Binary {
   //...
   friend ostream& operator << (ostream&,
   Binary&);
};
ostream& operator << (ostream &os, Binary
   &n)
{
   char str[binSize + 1];
   strncpy(str, n.bits, binSize);
```

```
    str[binSize] = '\0';
    cout << str;
    return os;
}
```

Given this definition, << can be used for the output of binary numbers in a manner identical to its use for the built-in types. For example,

```
Binary n1 = "01011", n2 = "11010";
cout << n1 << " + " << n1 << " = " << n1 + n2
    << '\n';
```

*will produce the following output:*

```
0000000000001011 + 0000000000011010 =
0000000000100101
```

In addition to its simplicity and elegance, this style of output eliminates the burden of remembering the name of the output function for each user-defined type.

Without the use of overloaded <<, the last example would have to be written as (assuming that \n has been removed from Print):

```
Binary n1 = "01011", n2 = "11010";
n1.Print(); cout << " + "; n2.Print();
cout << " = "; (n1 + n2).Print(); cout <<
    '\n';
```

## OVERLOADING >> FOR INPUT

Input of user-defined types is facilitated by overloading the >> operator, in a manner similar to the way << is overloaded. For any given user-defined type T, we can define an operator>> function which inputs objects of type T:

```
istream& operator >> (istream&, T&);
```

The first parameter must be a reference to istream so that multiple uses of >> can be concatenated. The second parameter must be a reference, since it will be modified by the function. Continuing with the Binary class example, we overload the >> operator for the input of bit streams. Again, because the first operand of >> must be an istream object, it cannot be overloaded as a member function:

```
class Binary {
   //...
   friend istream& operator >> (istream&,
   Binary&);
};
istream& operator >> (istream &is, Binary
   &n)
{
   char str[binSize + 1];
   cin >> str;
   n = Binary(str);//use the constructor for
   simplicity
   return is;
}
```

Given this definition, >> can be used for the input of binary numbers in a manner identical to its use for the built-in types. For example,

```
Binary n;
cin >> n;
```

will read a binary number from the keyboard into to n.

## OVERLOADING

Listing 7.27 defines a simple associative vector class. An associative vector is a one-dimensional array in which elements can be looked up by their contents rather than their position in the array. In AssocVec, each element has a string name (via which it can be looked up) and an associated integer value.

### Listing 7.27

```
#include <iostream.h>
#include <string.h>
class AssocVec {
public:
         AssocVec (const int dim);
         ~AssocVec (void);
   int& operator [] (const char *idx);
private:
   struct VecElem {
```

```
        char *index;
        int value;
    } *elems;   //vector elements
    int dim;    //vector dimension
    int used;   //elements used so far
};
```

## Annotation

5 The constructor creates an associative vector of the dimension specified by its argument.

7 The overloaded [] operator is used for accessing vector elements. The function which overloads [] must have exactly one parameter. Given a string index, it searches the vector for a match. If a matching index is found then a reference to its associated value is returned. Otherwise, a new element is created and a reference to this value is returned.

12 The vector elements are represented by a dynamic array of VecElem structures. Each vector element consists of a string (denoted by index) and an integer value (denoted by value).

The implementation of the member functions is as follows:

```
AssocVec::AssocVec (const int dim)
{
    AssocVec::dim = dim;
    used = 0;
    elems = new VecElem[dim];
}
AssocVec::~AssocVec (void)
{
    for (register i = 0; i < used; ++i)
          delete elems[i].index;
    delete [] elems;
}
int& AssocVec::operator [] (const char *idx)
{
    for (register i = 0; i < used; ++i)    /
    /search existing
```

```
elements
          if  (strcmp(idx,elems[i].index)  ==
   0)
                return  elems[i].value;
   if (used < dim &&       //create    new
   element
         (elems[used].index    =    new
   char[strlen(idx)+1]) != 0) {
         strcpy(elems[used].index,idx);
         elems[used].value = used + 1;
         return  elems[used++].value;
   }
   static int dummy = 0;
   return dummy;
}
```

Note that, because AssocVec::operator[] must return a valid reference, a reference to a dummy static integer is returned when the vector is full or when new fails. A reference expression is an lvalue and hence can appear on both sides of an assignment. If a function returns a reference then a call to that function can be assigned to. This is why the return type of AssocVec::operator[] is defined to be a reference. Using AssocVec we can now create associative vectors that behave very much like normal vectors:

```
AssocVec count(5);
count["apple"] = 5;
count["orange"] = 10;
count["fruit"]  =  count["apple"]  +
   count["orange"];
```

This will set count["fruit"] to 15.

## OVERLOADING ()

Listing 7.28 defines a matrix class. A matrix is a table of values (very similar to a two-dimensional array) whose size is denoted by the number of rows and columns in the table. An example of a simple 2 x 3 matrix would be:

$$M = \begin{bmatrix} 10 & 20 & 30 \\ 21 & 52 & 19 \end{bmatrix}$$

The standard mathematical notation for referring to matrix elements uses brackets. For example, element 20 of *M* (*i.e.*, in the first row and second column) is referred to as *M*(1,2). Matrix algebra provides a set of operations for manipulating matrices, which includes addition, subtraction, and multiplication.

**Listing 7.28**

```
1  #include <iostream.h>
2  class Matrix {
3  public:
4          Matrix (const short rows, const short cols);
5          ~Matrix (void) {delete elems;}
6      double& operator () (const short row, const short col);
7  friend ostream& operator << (ostream&, Matrix&);
8  friend Matrix operator + (Matrix&, Matrix&);
9  friend Matrix operator - (Matrix&, Matrix&);
10 friend Matrix operator * (Matrix&, Matrix&);
11 private:
12         const short rows;  //matrix rows
13         const short cols;  //matrix columns
14         double *elems;     //matrix elements
15 };
```

**Annotation**

4 The constructor creates a matrix of the size specified by its arguments, all of whose elements are initialized to 0.

6 The overloaded () operator is used for accessing matrix elements. The function which overloads () may have zero or more parameters. It returns a reference to the specified element's value.

7 The overloaded << is used for printing a matrix in tabular form.

8-10 These overloaded operators provide basic matrix operations.

14 The matrix elements are represented by a dynamic array of doubles.

The implementation of the first three member functions is as follows:

```
Matrix::Matrix (const short r, const short
   c): rows(r), cols(c)
{
   elems = new double[rows * cols];
}
double& Matrix::operator () (const short row,
   const short col)
{
   static double dummy = 0.0;
   return (row >= 1 && row <= rows && col >=
   1 && col <= cols)
         ? elems[(row - 1)*cols + (col - 1)]
         : dummy;
}
ostream& operator << (ostream &os, Matrix
   &m)
{
   for (register r = 1; r <= m.rows; ++r) {
         for (int c = 1; c <= m.cols; ++c)
               os << m(r,c) << " ";
         os << '\n';
   }
   return os;
}
```

As before, because Matrix::operator() must return a valid reference, a reference to a dummy static double is returned when the specified element does not exist. The following code fragment illustrates that matrix elements are lvalues:

```
Matrix m(2,3);
m(1,1) = 10;  m(1,2) = 20;   m(1,3) = 30;
m(2,1) = 15;  m(2,2) = 25;   m(2,3) = 35;
cout << m << '\n';
```

*This will produce the following output:*

```
10 20 30
15 25 35
```

## MEMBERWISE INITIALIZATION

Consider the following definition of the overloaded + operator for Matrix:

```
Matrix operator + (Matrix &p, Matrix &q)
{
    Matrix m(p.rows, p.cols);
    if (p.rows == q.rows && p.cols == q.cols)
          for (register r = 1; r <= p.rows;
    ++r)
                for (register c = 1; c <=
    p.cols; ++c)
                      m(r,c) = p(r,c) +
    q(r,c);
    return m;
}
```

This function returns a matrix object which is initialized to m. The initialization is handled by an internal constructor which the compiler automatically generates for Matrix:

```
Matrix::Matrix (const Matrix &m):
    rows(m.rows), cols(m.cols)
{
    elems = m.elems;
}
```

This form of initialization is called memberwise initialization because the special constructor initializes the object member by member.

If the data members of the object being initialized are themselves objects of another class, then those are also memberwise initialized, etc. As a result of the default memberwise initialization, the elems data member of both objects will point to the same dynamically-allocated block.

However, m is destroyed upon the function returning. Hence the destructor deletes the block pointed to by m.elems, leaving the returned object's elems data member pointing to an invalid block! This ultimately leads to a runtime failure (typically a bus error).

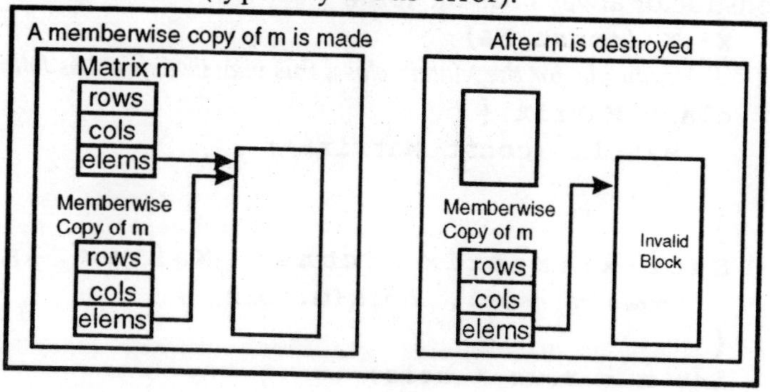


Fig. 7.11 The Danger of the Default Memberwise Initialization of Objects with Pointers.

*Memberwise initialization occurs in the following situations*:

- When defining and initializing an object in a declaration statement that uses another object as its initializer, *e.g.*, Matrix n = m in Foo below.
- When passing an object argument to a function (not applicable to a reference or pointer argument), *e.g.*, m in Foo below.
- When returning an object value from a function (not applicable to a reference or pointer return value), *e.g.*, return n in Foo below.

```
Matrix Foo (Matrix m)//memberwise copy
   argument to m
{
   Matrix n = m;//memberwise copy m to n
   //...
   return n;//memberwise copy n and return
   copy
}
```

It should be obvious that default memberwise initialization is generally adequate for classes which have no pointer data members (*e.g.*, Point). The problems caused by the default memberwise initialization of other classes can be avoided by explicitly defining the constructor in charge of memberwise initialization. For any given class X, the constructor always has the form:

```
X::X (const X&);
```

*For example, for the Matrix class, this may be defined as follows:*

```
class Matrix {
   Matrix (const Matrix&);
   //...
};
Matrix::Matrix  (const  Matrix  &m):
   rows(m.rows), cols(m.cols)
{
int n = rows * cols;
elems = new double[n];                    //
   same size
for (register i = 0; i < n; ++i)          //
   copy elements
   elems[i] = m.elems[i];
}
```

## MEMBERWISE ASSIGNMENT

Objects of the same class are assigned to one another by an internal overloading of the = operator which is automatically generated by the compiler. For example, to handle the assignment in

```
Matrix m(2,2), n(2,2);
//...
m = n;
```

the compiler automatically generates the following internal function:

```
Matrix& Matrix::operator = (const Matrix &m)
{
   rows = m.rows;
   cols = m.cols;
   elems = m.elems;
}
```

This is identical in its approach to memberwise initialization and is called memberwise assignment. It suffers from exactly the same problems, which in turn can be overcome by explicitly overloading the = operator. For example, for the Matrix class, the following overloading of = would be appropriate:

```
Matrix& Matrix::operator = (const Matrix &m)
{
    if (rows == m.rows && cols == m.cols) {/
    /must match
            int n = rows * cols;
            for (register i = 0; i < n; ++i)//
    copy elements
                    elems[i] = m.elems[i];
    }
    return *this;
}
```

In general, for any given class X, the = operator is overloaded by the following member of X:

```
X& X::operator = (X&)
```

Operator = can only be overloaded as a member, and not globally.

## OVERLOADING NEW AND DELETE

Objects of different classes usually have different sizes and frequency of usage. As a result, they impose different memory requirements.

Small objects, in particular, are not efficiently handled by the default versions of new and delete. Every block allocated by new carries some overhead used for housekeeping purposes. For large objects this is not significant, but for small objects the overhead may be even bigger than the block itself. In addition, having too many small blocks can severely slow down subsequent allocation and deallocation.

The performance of a programme that dynamically creates many small objects can be significantly improved by usinga simpler memory management strategy for those objects. The dynamic storage management operators new and delete can be overloaded for a class, in which case they override the global definition of these operators when used for objects of that class.

As an example, suppose we wish to overload new and delete for the Point class, so that Point objects are allocated from an array:

```
#include <stddef.h>
#include <iostream.h>
const int maxPoints = 512;
class Point {
public:
   //...
   void* operator new     (size_t bytes);
   void operator delete   (void *ptr, size_t
   bytes);
private:
   int xVal, yVal;
   static union Block {
         int xy[2];
         Block *next;
   }                  *blocks;    //points to
   our freestore
   static Block       *freeList; //free-list
   of linked blocks
   static int         used;       //blocks
   used so far
};
```

The type name size_t is defined in stddef.h. New should always return a void*. The parameter of new denotes the size of the block to be allocated (in bytes). The corresponding argument is always automatically passed by the compiler. The first parameter of delete denotes the block to be deleted. The second parameter is optional and denotes the size of the allocated block. The corresponding arguments are automatically passed by the compiler.

Since blocks, freeList and used are static they do not affect the size of a Point object (it is still two integers). These are initialized as follows:

```
Point::Block *Point::blocks = new
   Block[maxPoints];
Point::Block *Point::freeList = 0;
```

```
int                Point::used = 0;
```

New takes the next available block from blocks and returns its address. Delete frees a block by inserting it in front of the linked-list denoted by freeList. When used reaches maxPoints, new removes and returns the first block in the linked-list, but fails (returns 0) when the linked-list is empty:

```
void* Point::operator new (size_t bytes)
{
   Block *res = freeList;
   return used < maxPoints
         ? &(blocks[used++])
         : (res == 0 ? 0
               : (freeList = freeList->next,
   res));
}
void Point::operator delete (void *ptr, size_t
   bytes)
{
   ((Block*) ptr)->next = freeList;
   freeList = (Block*) ptr;
}
```

Point::operator new and Point::operator delete are invoked *only* for Point objects. Calling new with any other type as argument will invoke the global definition of new, even if the call occurs inside a member function of Point.

*For example:*

```
Point *pt = new Point(1,1);      //calls
   Point::operator new
char *str = new char[10];        /          /
   calls::operator new
delete pt;                       //calls
   Point::operator delete
delete str;                      /          /
   calls::operator delete
```

Even when new and delete are overloaded for a class, global new and delete are used when creating anu destroying object arrays:

```
Point *points = new Point[5];   /          /
```

```
   calls::operator new
//...
delete [] points;                    /          /
   calls::operator delete
```

The functions which overload new and delete for a class are always assumed by the compiler to be static, which means that they will not have access to the this pointer and therefore the nonstatic class members. This is because when these operators are invoked for an object of the class, the object does not exist: new is invoked *before* the object is constructed, and delete is called *after* it has been destroyed.

## OVERLOADING ->, *, AND &

It is possible to divert the flow of control to a user-defined function before a pointer to an object is dereferenced using -> or *, or before the address of an object is obtained using &. This can be used to do some extra pointer processing, and is facilitated by overloading unary operators ->, *, and &.

For classes that do not overload ->, this operator is always binary: the left operand is a pointer to a class object and the right operand is a class member name. When the left operand of -> is an object or reference of type X (but not pointer), X is expected to have overloaded -> as unary.

In this case, -> is first applied to the left operand to produce a result p. If p is a pointer to a class Y then p is used as the left operand of binary -> and the right operand is expected to be a member of Y. Otherwise, p is used as the left operand of unary -> and the whole procedure is repeated for class Y. Consider the following classes that overload ->:

```
class A {
   //...
   B& operator -> (void);
};
class B {
   //...
   Point* operator -> (void);
};
```

The effect of applying -> to an object of type A

```
A obj;
int i = obj->xVal;
```

is the successive application of overloaded -> in A and B:

```
int i = (B::operator->(A::operator->(obj)))-
   >xVal;
```

In other words, A::operator-> is applied to obj to give p, B::operator-> is applied to p to give q, and since q is a pointer to Point, the final result is q- >xVal. Unary operators * and & can also be overloaded so that the semantic correspondence between ->, *, and & is preserved. As an example, consider a library system which represents a book record as a raw string of the following format:

```
"%Aauthor\0%Ttitle\0%Ppublisher\0%Ccity
\0%Vvolume  \0%Yyear\0\n"
```

Each field starts with a field specifier (*e.g.*, %A specifies an author) and ends with a null character (*i.e.*, \0). The fields can appear in any order. Also, some fields may be missing from a record, in which case a default value must be used. For efficiency reasons we may want to keep the data in this format but use the following structure whenever we need to access the fields of a record:

```
struct Book {
   char *raw;        //raw format (kept for
   reference)
   char *author;
   char *title;
   char *publisher;
   char *city;
   short vol;
   short year;
};
```

*The default field values are denoted by a global Book variable*:

```
Book defBook = {
"raw", "Author?", "Title?", "Publisher?",
   "City?", 0, 0
};
```

We now define a class for representing raw records, and overload the unary pointer operators to map a raw record to a Book structure whenever necessary.

```
#include <iostream.h>
#include <stdlib.h> //needed for atoi()
   below
int const cacheSize = 10;
class RawBook {
public:
         RawBook (char *str) {data = str;}
   Book* operator -> (void);
   Book& operator * (void);
   Book* operator & (void);
private:
   Book* RawToBook (void);
   char *data;
   static Book *cache;     //cache memory
   static short curr;      //current record
   in cache
   static short used;      //number of used
   cache records
};
```

To reduce the frequency of mappings from RawBook to Book, we have used a simple cache memory of 10 records. The corresponding static members are initialized as follows:

```
Book *RawBook::cache = new Book[cacheSize];
short RawBook::curr = 0;
short RawBook::used = 0;
```

The private member function RawToBook searches the cache for a RawBook and returns a pointer to its corresponding Book structure. If the book is not in the cache, RawToBook loads the book at the current position in the cache:

```
Book* RawBook::RawToBook (void)
{
   char *str = data;
   for (register i = 0; i < used; ++i)
   //search cache
         if (data == cache[i].raw)
               return cache + i;
   curr = used < cacheSize ? used++//update
   curr and used
```

```
: (curr < 9 ? ++curr: 0);
Book *bk = cache + curr;                    //the
book
*bk = defBook;                              //set
default values
bk->raw = data;
for (;;) {
      while (*str++ != '%')                 /   /
skip to next specifier
      ;
      switch (*str++) {                     //get
a field
case 'A': bk->author = str; break;
case 'T': bk->title = str; break;
case 'P': bk->publisher = str; break;
case 'C': bk->city = str; break;
case 'V': bk->vol = atoi(str); break;
case 'Y': bk->year = atoi(str); break;
}
while (*str++ != '\0') //skip till end of
field
;
if (*str == '\n') break;      //end   of
record
}
return bk;
}
```

The overloaded operators ->, *, and & are easily defined in terms of

*Raw to book*:

```
Book* RawBook::operator -> (void) {return
RawToBook();}
Book& RawBook::operator * (void) {return
*RawToBook();}
Book* RawBook::operator & (void) {return
RawToBook();}
```

The identical definitions for -> and & should not be surprising since -> is unary in this context and semantically equivalent to &. The following test case demonstrates that the operators behave as expected. It sets up two book records and prints each using different operators.

```
main ()
{
    RawBook  r1("%AA.  Peters\0%TBlue
    Earth\0%PPhedra\0%CSydney\0%
                Y1981\0\n");
    RawBook      r2("%TPregnancy\0%AF.
    Jackson\0%Y1987\0%PMiles\0\n");
    cout  << r1->author << ", " << r1->title
    << ", "
    << r1->publisher << ", " << r1->city <<
    ", "
    << (*r1).vol << ", " << (*r1).year <<
    '\n';
    Book *bp = &r2;//note use of &
    cout  << bp->author << ", " << bp->title
    << ", "
    << bp->publisher << ", " << bp->city <<
    ", "
    << bp->vol << ", " << bp->year << '\n';
}
```

*It will produce the following output:*

```
A. Peters, Blue Earth, Phedra, Sydney, 0,
   1981
F. Jackson, Pregnancy, Miles, City?, 0, 1987
```

## OVERLOADING ++ AND –

The auto increment and auto decrement operators can be overloaded in both prefix and postfix form. To distinguish between the two, the postfix version is specified to take an extra integer argument. For example, the prefix and postfix versions of ++ may be overloaded for the Binary class as follows:

```
class Binary {
    //...
    friend Binary operator ++ (Binary&);
```

```
    //prefix
    friend Binary operator ++ (Binary&, int);
    //postfix
};
```

Although we have chosen to define these as global friend functions, they can also be defined as member functions. Both are easily defined in terms of the + operator defined earlier:

```
Binary operator ++ (Binary &n) //prefix
{
    return n = n + Binary(1);
}
Binary operator ++ (Binary &n, int)  /   /
    postfix
{
    Binary m = n;
    n = n + Binary(1);
    return m;
}
```

Note that we have simply ignored the extra parameter of the postfix version. When this operator is used, the compiler automatically supplies a default argument for it. The following code fragment exercises both versions of the operator:

```
Binary n1 = "01011";
Binary n2 = "11010";
cout << ++n1 << '\n';
cout << n2++ << '\n';
cout << n2 << '\n';
```

It will produce the following output:

```
0000000000001100
0000000000011010
0000000000011011
```

The prefix and postfix versions of — may be overloaded in exactly the same way.

## QUESTIONS

Q1. Write overloaded versions of a Max function which compares two integers, two reals, or two strings, and returns the 'larger' one.

Q2. Overload the following two operators for the Set class:

- Operator - which gives the difference of two sets (*e.g.* *s* - *t* gives a set consisting of those elements of *s* which are not in *t*).
- Operator <= which checks if a set is contained by another (*e.g.*, *s* <= *t* is true if all the elements of *s* are also in *t*).

Q3. Overload the following two operators for the Binary class:

- Operator - which gives the difference of two binary values. For simplicity, assume that the first operand is always greater than the second operand.
- Operator [] which indexes a bit by its position and returns its value as a 0 or 1 integer.

Q4. Sparse matrices are used in a number of numerical methods (*e.g.*, finite element analysis). A sparse matrix is one which has the great majority of its elements set to zero. In practice, sparse matrices of sizes up to 500 × 500 are not uncommon. On a machine which uses a 64-bit representation for reals, storing such a matrix as an array would require 2 megabytes of storage. A more economic representation would record only nonzero elements together with their positions in the matrix. Define a SparseMatrix class which uses a linked-list to record only nonzero elements, and overload the +, –, and * operators for it. Also define an appropriate memberwise initialization constructor and memberwise assignment operator for the class.

Q5. Complete the implementation of the following String class. Note that two versions of the constructor and = are required, one for initializing/assigning to a String using a char*, and one for memberwise initialization/assignment. Operator [] should index a string character using its position. Operator + should concatenate two strings.

```
class String {
public:
            String      (const char*);
```

```
            String    (const String&);
            String    (const short);
            ~String   (void);

String&     operator = (const char*);
String&     operator = (const String&);
char&            operator [] (const short);
int         Length           ( v o i d )
  {return(len);}
friend String  operator + ( c o n s t
  String&, const String&);
friend ostream& operator << (o s t r e a m & ,
  String&);
private:
   char         *chars;     / / s t r i n g
  characters
   short        len;        //length  of
  string
   };
```

Q6. A bit vector is a vector with binary elements, that is, each element is either a 0 or a 1. Small bit vectors are conveniently represented by unsigned integers. For example, an unsigned char can represent a bit vector of 8 elements. Larger bit vectors can be defined as arrays of such smaller bit vectors. Complete the implementation of the Bitvec class, as defined below. It should allow bit vectors of any size to be created and manipulated using the associated operators.

```
enum Bool {false, true};
typedef unsigned char uchar;
class BitVec {
public:
   BitVec  (const short dim);
   BitVec  (const char* bits);
   BitVec  (const BitVec&);
   ~BitVec (void) {delete vec;}
   BitVec& operator =   (const BitVec&);
   BitVec& operator &=  (const BitVec&);
```

```
        BitVec& operator |=  (const BitVec&);
        BitVec& operator ^=  (const BitVec&);
        BitVec& operator <<= (const short);
        BitVec& operator >>= (const short);
    intoperator [] (const short idx);
    void Set (const shortidx);
    void Reset (const short idx);
        BitVec operator ~  (void);
        BitVec operator &  (const BitVec&);
        BitVec operator |  (const BitVec&);
        BitVec operator ^  (const BitVec&);
        BitVec operator << (const short n);
        BitVec operator >> (const short n);
        Bool operator == (const BitVec&);
        Bool operator != (const BitVec&);
        friend ostream& operator << (ostream&,
      BitVec&);
    private:
        uchar *vec;     //vector of 8*bytes bits
        short bytes;    //bytes in the vector
    };
```

ANSWERS

1.
```
#include <string.h>
const int Max (const int x, const int y)
{
    return x >= y ? x: y;
}
const double Max (const double x, const double
    y)
{
    return x >= y ? x: y;
}
const char* Max (const char *x, const char
    *y)
{
    return strcmp(x,y) >= 0 ? x: y;
}
```

```
2. class Set {
       //...
       friend Set operator - (Set&, Set&);
       //difference
       friend Bool operator <= (Set&, Set&);
       //subset
       //...
   };
   Set operator - (Set &set1, Set &set2)
   {
      Set res;
      for (register i = 0; i < set1.card; ++i)
            if (!(set1.elems[i] & set2))
                  res.elems[res.card++] =
      set1.elems[i];
      return res;
   }
   Bool operator <= (Set &set1, Set &set2)
   {
      if (set1.card > set2.card)
            return false;
      for (register i = 0; i < set1.card; ++i)
            if (!(set1.elems[i] & set2))
                  return false;
      return true;
   }
3. class Binary {
   //...
   friend Binary operator - (const Binary,
      const Binary);
            int   operator [](const int n)
                  {return bits[15-n] == '1' ?
      1: 0;}
   //...
   };
   Binary operator - (const Binary n1, const
      Binary n2)
   {
```

```
unsigned borrow = 0;
unsigned value;
Binary res = "0";
      for (register i = 15; i >= 0; —i) {
            value =     (n1.bits[i] == '0'
? 0: 1) -
                  (n2.bits[i] == '0' ? 0:
1) + borrow;
            res.bits[i] = (value == -1 ||
value == 1 ? '1': '0');
            borrow = (value == -1 || borrow
!= 0 && value == 1 ? 1: 0);
      }
      return res;
}
```

4.
```
#include <iostream.h>
class Matrix {
public:
        Matrix (const int rows, const int
   cols);
        Matrix (const Matrix&);
        ~Matrix (void);
   double& operator () (const int row, const
   int col);
   Matrix& operator = (const Matrix&);
friend ostream& operator << (ostream&,
   Matrix&);
friend Matrix operator + (Matrix&, Matrix&);
friend Matrix operator - (Matrix&, Matrix&);
friend Matrix operator * (Matrix&, Matrix&);
        int Rows (void) {return rows;}
        int Cols (void) {return cols;}
protected:
   class Element {              //nonzero
   element
   public:
              Element (const int row, const
   int col, double);
```

```
        const int Row (void) {return row;}
        const int Col (void) {return col;}
        double& Value (void) {return value;}
        Element*& Next (void) {return next;}
        Element* CopyList(Element *list);
        void DeleteList (Element *list);
    private:
    const int row, col;    //row and column
    of element
    double value;          //element value
    Element *next;         //pointer to next
    element
    };
    double& InsertElem (Element *elem, const
    int row, const int
col);
    int rows, cols;                //matrix
    dimensions
    Element *elems;                //linked-
    list of elements
};
Matrix::Element::Element (const int r, const
    int c, double val)
        : row(r), col(c)
{
    value = val;
    next = 0;
}
Matrix::Element* Matrix::Element::CopyList
    (Element *list)
{
    Element *prev = 0;
    Element *first = 0;
    Element *copy;
    for (; list != 0; list = list->Next()) {
        copy = new Element(list->Row(),
    list->Col(), list->Value());
        if (prev == 0)
```

```
            first = copy;
        else
            prev->Next() = copy;
        prev = copy;
    }
    return first;
}
void Matrix::Element::DeleteList (Element
    *list)
{
    Element *next;
    for (; list != 0; list = next) {
        next = list->Next();
        delete list;
    }
}
//InsertElem creates a new element and inserts
    it before
//or after the element denoted by elem.
double& Matrix::InsertElem (Element *elem,
    const int row, constint col)
{
    Element* newElem = new Element(row, col,
    0.0);
    if (elem == elems && (elems == 0 || row <
    elems->Row() ||
                    row == elems->Row() &&
    col < elems->Col())) {
        //insert in front of the list:
        newElem->Next() = elems;
        elems = newElem;
    } else {
        //insert after elem:
        newElem->Next() = elem->Next();
        elem->Next() = newElem;
    }
    return newElem->Value();
}
```

```
Matrix::Matrix (const int rows, const int
   cols)
{
   Matrix::rows = rows;
   Matrix::cols = cols;
   elems = 0;
}
Matrix::Matrix (const Matrix &m)
{
   rows = m.rows;
   cols = m.cols;
   elems = m.elems->CopyList(m.elems);
}
Matrix::~Matrix (void)
{
   elems->DeleteList(elems);
}
Matrix& Matrix::operator = (const Matrix &m)
{
   elems->DeleteList(elems);
   rows = m.rows;
   cols = m.cols;
   elems = m.elems->CopyList(m.elems);
   return *this;
}
double& Matrix::operator () (const int row,
   const int col)
{
   if (elems == 0 || row < elems->Row() ||
         row == elems->Row() && col < elems-
   >Col())
         //create an element and insert in
   front:
         return InsertElem(elems, row, col);
   //check if it's the first element in the
   list:
   if (row == elems->Row() && col == elems-
   >Col())
```

```
        return elems->Value();
    //search the rest of the list:
    for (Element *elem = elems; elem->Next()
    != 0; elem = elem->Next())
        if (row == elem->Next()->Row()) {
            if (col == elem->Next()-
    >Col())
                return elem->Next()-
    >Value(); //found it!
            else if (col < elem->Next()-
    >Col())
                break;//doesn't exist
        } else if (row < elem->Next()->Row())
            break;//doesn't exist
    //create new element and insert just after
    elem:
    return InsertElem(elem, row, col);
}
ostream& operator << (ostream &os, Matrix
    &m)
{
        Matrix::Element *elem = m.elems;
        for (register row = 1; row <= m.rows;
    ++row) {
            for (register col = 1; col <=
    m.cols; ++col)
                if (elem != 0 && elem-
    >Row() == row && elem->Col() == col)
{
                os << elem->Value() <<
    '\t';
                elem = elem->Next();
            } else
                os << 0.0 << '\t';
        os << '\n';
    }
    return os;
}
```

```
Matrix operator + (Matrix &p, Matrix &q)
{
Matrix m(p.rows, q.cols);
   //copy p:
   for (Matrix::Element *pe = p.elems; pe !=
   0; pe = pe->Next())
         m(pe->Row(), pe->Col()) = pe-
   >Value();
   //add q:
   for (Matrix::Element *qe = q.elems; qe !=
   0; qe = qe->Next())
         m(qe->Row(), qe->Col()) += qe-
   >Value();
   return m;
}
Matrix operator - (Matrix &p, Matrix &q)
{
   Matrix m(p.rows, q.cols);
   //copy p:
   for (Element *pe = p.elems; pe != 0; pe =
   pe->Next())
         m(pe->Row(), pe->Col()) = pe-
   >Value();
   //subtract q:
   for (Element *qe = q.elems; qe != 0; qe =
   qe->Next())
         m(qe->Row(), qe->Col()) -= qe-
   >Value();
   return m;
}
Matrix operator * (Matrix &p, Matrix &q)
{
   Matrix m(p.rows, q.cols);
   for (Element *pe = p.elems; pe != 0; pe =
   pe->Next())
         for (Element *qe = q.elems; qe !=
   0; qe = qe->Next())
               if (pe->Col() == qe->Row())
```

```
          m(pe->Row(),qe->Col()) += pe-
    >Value() * qe->Value();
    return m;
  }
5. #include <string.h>
   #include <iostream.h>
   class String {
   public:
          String      (const char*);
          String      (const String&);
          String      (const short);
          ~String     (void);
     String&    operator = (const char*);
     String&    operator = (const String&);
     char& operator [] (const short);
     int   Length      (void) {return(len);}
     friend String   operator + ( c o n s t
     String&, const String&);
     friend ostream& operator << (ostream&,
     String&);
   protected:
     char  *chars;      //string characters
     short len;         //length of chars
   };
   String::String (const char *str)
   {
     len = strlen(str);
     chars = new char[len + 1];
     strcpy(chars, str);
   }
   String::String (const String &str)
   {
     len = str.len;
     chars = new char[len + 1];
     strcpy(chars, str.chars);
   }
   String::String (const short size)
   {
```

```
    len = size;
    chars = new char[len + 1];
    chars[0] = '\0';
}
String::~String (void)
{
    delete chars;
}
String& String::operator = (const char *str)
{
    short strLen = strlen(str);
    if (len != strLen) {
          delete chars;
          len = strLen;
          chars = new char[strLen + 1];
    }
    strcpy(chars, str);
    return(*this);
}
String& String::operator = (const String &str)
{
          if (this != &str) {
                if (len != str.len) {
                delete chars;
                len = str.len;
                chars = new char[str.len + 1];
          }
          strcpy(chars, str.chars);
    }
    return(*this);
}
char& String::operator [] (const short index)
{
    static char dummy = '\0';
    return(index >= 0 && index < len ?
    chars[index]: dummy);
}
String operator + (const String &str1, const
```

```
    String &str2)
{
    String result(str1.len + str2.len);
    strcpy(result.chars, str1.chars);
    strcpy(result.chars + str1.len,
    str2.chars);
    return(result);
}
ostream& operator << (ostream &out, String
    &str)
{
    out << str.chars;
    return(out);
}
```

6.
```
#include <string.h>
#include <iostream.h>
enum Bool {false, true};
typedef unsigned char uchar;
class BitVec {
public:
        BitVec    (const short dim);
        BitVec    (const char* bits);
        BitVec    (const BitVec&);
        ~BitVec   (void) {delete vec;}
    BitVec&   operator = (const BitVec&);
    BitVec&   operator &=(const BitVec&);
    BitVec&   operator |=(const BitVec&);
    BitVec&   operator ^=(const BitVec&);
    BitVec&   operator <<=    ( c o n s t
    short);
    BitVec&   operator >>=    ( c o n s t
    short);
    int       operator [] (const short idx);
    void  Set        (const short idx);
    void  Reset (const short idx);
    BitVec    operator ~ ();
    BitVec    operator & (const BitVec&);
    BitVec    operator | (const BitVec&);
```

```
   BitVec     operator ^ (const BitVec&);
   BitVec     operator <<(const short n);
   BitVec     operator >>(const short n);
   Bool  operator ==(const BitVec&);
   Bool  operator !=(const BitVec&);
friend ostream& operator << (ostream&,
   BitVec&);
protected:
uchar *vec;          //vector of 8*bytes bits
short bytes;  //bytes in the vector
};
//set the bit denoted by idx to 1
inline void BitVec::Set (const short idx)
{
   vec[idx/8] |= (1 << idx%8);
}
//reset the bit denoted by idx to 0
inline void BitVec::Reset (const short idx)
{
vec[idx/8] &= ~(1 << idx%8);
}
inline BitVec& BitVec::operator &= (const
   BitVec &v)
{
   return (*this) = (*this) & v;
}
inline BitVec& BitVec::operator |= (const
   BitVec &v)
{
   return (*this) = (*this) | v;
}
inline BitVec& BitVec::operator ^= (const
   BitVec &v)
{
   return (*this) = (*this) ^ v;
}
inline BitVec& BitVec::operator <<= (const
   short n)
```

```
{
   return (*this) = (*this) << n;
}
inline BitVec& BitVec::operator >>= (const
   short n)
{
   return (*this) = (*this) >> n;
}
//return the bit denoted by idx
inline int BitVec::operator [] (const short
   idx)
{
   return vec[idx/8] & (1 << idx%8) ? true:
   false;
}
inline Bool BitVec::operator != (const BitVec
   &v)
{
   return *this == v ? false: true;
}
BitVec::BitVec (const short dim)
{
   bytes = dim/8 + (dim % 8 == 0 ? 0: 1);
   vec = new uchar[bytes];
   for (register i = 0; i < bytes; ++i)
   vec[i] = 0;       //all bits are initially
   zero
}
BitVec::BitVec (const char *bits)
{
   int len = strlen(bits);
   bytes = len/8 + (len % 8 == 0 ? 0: 1);
   vec = new uchar[bytes];
   for (register i = 0; i < bytes; ++i)
         vec[i] = 0;       //initialize all
   bits to zero
   for (i = len - 1; i >= 0; —i)
         if (*bits++ == '1')//set the 1 bits
```

```
                vec[i/8] |= (1 << (i%8));
}
BitVec::BitVec (const BitVec &v)
{
   bytes = v.bytes;
   vec = new uchar[bytes];
   for (register i = 0; i < bytes; ++i)//
   copy bytes
   vec[i] = v.vec[i];
}
BitVec& BitVec::operator = (const BitVec&
   v)
{
   for (register i = 0; i < (v.bytes < bytes
   ? v.bytes: bytes); ++i)
         vec[i] = v.vec[i];//copy bytes
   for (; i < bytes; ++i)//extra bytes in
   *this
         vec[i] = 0;
   return *this;
}
//bitwise COMPLEMENT
BitVec BitVec::operator ~ (void)
{
   BitVec r(bytes * 8);
   for (register i = 0; i < bytes; ++i)
         r.vec[i] = ~vec[i];
   return r;
}
//bitwise AND
BitVec BitVec::operator & (const BitVec &v)
{
   BitVec r((bytes > v.bytes ? bytes: v.bytes)
   * 8);
   for (register i = 0; i < (bytes < v.bytes
   ? bytes: v.bytes); ++i)
         r.vec[i] = vec[i] & v.vec[i];
   return r;
```

```
}
//bitwise OR
BitVec BitVec::operator | (const BitVec &v)
{
   BitVec r((bytes > v.bytes ? bytes: v.bytes)
   * 8);
   for (register i = 0; i < (bytes < v.bytes
   ? bytes: v.bytes); ++i)
        r.vec[i] = vec[i] | v.vec[i];
   return r;
}
//bitwise exclusive-OR
BitVec BitVec::operator ^ (const BitVec &v)
{
   BitVec r((bytes > v.bytes ? bytes: v.bytes)
   * 8);
   for (register i = 0; i < (bytes < v.bytes
   ? bytes: v.bytes); ++i)
        r.vec[i] = vec[i] ^ v.vec[i];
   return r;
}
//SHIFT LEFT by n bits
BitVec BitVec::operator << (const short n)
{
   BitVec r(bytes * 8);
   int   zeros = n/8;     //bytes on the
   left to become zero
   int   shift = n % 8;  //left shift for
   remaining bytes
   register i;
for (i = bytes - 1; i >= zeros; —i)//shift
   bytes left
   r.vec[i] = vec[i - zeros];
for (; i >= 0; —i)//zero left bytes
   r.vec[i] = 0;
unsigned char prev = 0;
for (i = zeros; i < r.bytes; ++i) {//shift
   bits left
```

```
    r.vec[i] = (r.vec[i] << shift) | prev;
    prev = vec[i - zeros] >> (8 - shift);
}
return r;
}
//SHIFT RIGHT by n bits
BitVec BitVec::operator >> (const short n)
{
BitVec r(bytes * 8);
int           zeros = n/8;      //bytes on
    the right to become
zero
int           shift = n % 8;    / / r i g h t
    shift for remaining bytes
register i;
for (i = 0; i < bytes - zeros; ++i) /   /
    shift bytes right
    r.vec[i] = vec[i + zeros];
for (; i < bytes; ++i)//zero right bytes
    r.vec[i] = 0;
uchar prev = 0;
for (i = r.bytes - zeros - 1; i >= 0; –i) {/
    /shift bits right
    r.vec[i] = (r.vec[i] >> shift) | prev;
    prev = vec[i + zeros] << (8 - shift);
}
return r;
}
Bool BitVec::operator == (const BitVec &v)
{
    int          smaller = bytes < v.bytes ?
    bytes: v.bytes;
    register i;
    for (i = 0; i < smaller; ++i)//compare
    bytes
          if (vec[i] != v.vec[i])
                return false;
    for (i = smaller; i < bytes; ++i)//extra
```

```
   bytes in first operand
         if (vec[i] != 0)
               return false;
   for (i = smaller; i < v.bytes; ++i)//
   extra bytes in second
operand
   if (v.vec[i] != 0)
         return false;
return true;
}
ostream& operator << (ostream &os, BitVec
   &v)
{
   const int maxBytes = 256;
   char buf[maxBytes * 8 + 1];
   char *str = buf;
   int n = v.bytes > maxBytes ? maxBytes:
   v.bytes;
   for (register i = n-1; i >= 0; –i)
         for (register j = 7; j >= 0; –j)
               *str++ = v.vec[i] & (1 << j) ?
   '1': '0';
         *str = '\0';
         os << buf;
         return os;
}
```

# 6

# Structure of Programme

## INTRODUCTION

Probably the best way to start learning a programming language is by writing a programme. Therefore, here is our first programme:

```
// my first programme in C++
#include <iostream>
using namespace std;
int main ()
{
    cout << "Hello World!";
    return 0;
} Hello World!
```

The first panel shows the source code for our first programme. The second one shows the result of the programme once compiled and executed. The way to edit and compile a programme depends on the compiler you are using. Depending on whether it has a Development Interface or not and on its version. Consult the compilers section and the manual or help included with your compiler if you have doubts on how to compile a C++ console programme.

The previous programme is the typical programme that programmer apprentices write for the first time, and its result is the printing on screen of the "Hello World!" sentence. It is one of the simplest programmes that can be written in C++, but it already contains the fundamental components that every C++ programme has. We are going to look line by line at the code we have just written:

```
// my first programme in C++
```

This is a comment line. All lines beginning with two slash signs (//) are considered comments and do not have any effect on the behaviour of the programme. The programmer can use them to include short explanations or observations within the source code itself. In this case, the line is a brief description of what our programme is.

```
#include <iostream>
```

Lines beginning with a pound sign (#) are directives for the preprocessor. They are not regular code lines with expressions but indications for the compiler's preprocessor. In this case the directive #include <iostream> tells the preprocessor to include the iostream standard file. This specific file (iostream) includes the declarations of the basic standard input-output library in C++, and it is included because its functionality is going to be used later in the programme.

```
using namespace std;
```

All the elements of the standard C++ library are declared within what is called a namespace, the namespace with the name *std*. So in order to access its functionality we declare with this expression that we will be using these entities. This line is very frequent in C++ programmes that use the standard library, and in fact it will be included in most of the source codes included in these tutorials.

```
int main ()
```

This line corresponds to the beginning of the definition of the main function. The main function is the point by where all C++ programmes start their execution, independently of its location within the source code. It does not matter whether there are other functions with other names defined before or after it - the instructions contained within this function's definition will always be the first ones to be executed in any C++ programme. For that same reason, it is essential that all C++ programmes have a main function.

The word main is followed in the code by a pair of parentheses (()). That is because it is a function declaration: In C++, what differentiates a function declaration from other types of expressions are these parentheses that follow its name.

Optionally, these parentheses may enclose a list of parameters within them. Right after these parentheses we can find the body of the main function enclosed in braces ({}). What is contained within these braces is what the function does when it is executed.

```
cout << "Hello World";
```

This line is a C++ statement. A statement is a simple or compound expression that can actually produce some effect. In fact, this statement performs the only action that generates a visible effect in our first programme.

cout represents the standard output stream in C++, and the meaning of the entire statement is to insert a sequence of characters (in this case the Hello World sequence of characters) into the standard output stream (which usually is the screen).

cout is declared in the iostream standard file within the std namespace, so that's why we needed to include that specific file and to declare that we were going to use this specific namespace earlier in our code.

Notice that the statement ends with a semicolon character (;). This character is used to mark the end of the statement and in fact it must be included at the end of all expression statements in all C++ programmes (one of the most common syntax errors is indeed to forget to include some semicolon after a statement).

```
return 0;
```

The return statement causes the main function to finish. return may be followed by a return code (in our example is followed by the return code 0). A return code of 0 for the main function is generally interpreted as the programme worked as expected without any errors during its execution. This is the most usual way to end a C++ console programme.

You may have noticed that not all the lines of this programme perform actions when the code is executed. There were lines containing only comments (those beginning by //). There were lines with directives for the compiler's preprocessor (those beginning by #). Then there were lines that began the declaration of a function (in this case, the main function) and, finally lines with statements (like the insertion into cout), which were all included within the block delimited by the braces ({}) of the main function. The programme has been structured in different lines in order to be more readable, but in C++, we do not have strict rules on how to separate instructions in different lines. For example, instead of,

```
int main ()
{
    cout << " Hello World ";
    return 0;
}
```

We could have written:

```
int main () { cout << "Hello World"; return 0;
    }
```

All in just one line and this would have had exactly the same meaning as the previous code. In C++, the separation between statements is specified with an ending semicolon (;) at the end of each one, so the separation in different code lines does not matter at all for this purpose. We can write many statements per line or write a single statement that takes many code lines. The division of code in different lines serves only to make it more legible and schematic for the humans that may read it. Let us add an additional instruction to our first programme:

```
// my second programme in C++
#include <iostream>
using namespace std;
int main ()
{
    cout << "Hello World! ";
    cout << "I'm a C++ programme";
    return 0;
} Hello World! I'm a C++ programme
```

In this case, we performed two insertions into cout in two different statements. Once again, the separation in different lines of code has been done just to give greater readability to the programme, since main could have been perfectly valid defined this way:

```
int main () { cout << " Hello World! "; cout <<
    " I'm a C++ programme "; return 0; }
```

We were also free to divide the code into more lines if we considered it more convenient:

```
int main ()
{
    cout <<
        "Hello World!";
    cout
        << "I'm a C++ programme";
    return 0;
}
```

And the result would again have been exactly the same as in the previous examples. Preprocessor directives (those that begin by #) are out of this general rule since they are not statements. They are lines read and processed by the preprocessor and do not produce any code by themselves. Preprocessor directives must be specified in their own line and do not have to end with a semicolon (;).

## Comments

Comments are parts of the source code disregarded by the compiler. They simply do nothing. Their purpose is only to allow the programmer to insert notes or descriptions embedded within the source code.

*C++ supports two ways to insert comments*:

```
// line comment
/* block comment */
```

The first of them, known as line comment, discards everything from where the pair of slash signs (//) is found up to the end of that same line. The second one, known as block comment, discards everything between the /* characters and the first appearance of the */ characters, with the possibility of including more than one line.

*We are going to add comments to our second programme*:

```
/* my second programme in C++
 with more comments */
#include <iostream>
using namespace std;
int main ()
```

```
{
    cout << "Hello World! "; // prints Hello
    World!
    cout << "I'm a C++ programme"; // prints
    I'm a C++ programme
    return 0;
} Hello World! I'm a C++ programme
```

If you include comments within the source code of your programmes without using the comment characters combinations //, /* or */, the compiler will take them as if they were C++ expressions, most likely causing one or several error messages when you compile it.

## VARIABLES. DATA TYPES.

The usefulness of the "Hello World" programmes shown in the previous section is quite questionable. We had to write several lines of code, compile them, and then execute the resulting programme just to obtain a simple sentence written on the screen as result. It certainly would have been much faster to type the output sentence by ourselves. However, programming is not limited only to printing simple texts on the screen. In order to go a little further on and to become able to write programmes that perform useful tasks that really save us work we need to introduce the concept of variable.

Let us think that I ask you to retain the number 5 in your mental memory, and then I ask you to memorize also the number 2 at the same time. You have just stored two different values in your memory. Now, if I ask you to add 1 to the first number I said, you should be retaining the numbers 6 (that is 5+1) and 2 in your memory. Values that we could now for example subtract and obtain 4 as result. The whole process that you have just done with your mental memory is a simile of what a computer can do with two variables. The same process can be expressed in C++ with the following instruction set:

```
a = 5;
b = 2;
a = a + 1;
result = a - b;
```

Obviously, this is a very simple example since we have only used two small integer values, but consider that your computer can store millions of numbers like these at the same time and conduct sophisticated mathematical operations with them. Therefore, we can define a variable as a portion of memory to store a determined value. Each variable needs an identifier that distinguishes it from the others, for example, in the previous code the variable identifiers were a, b and result, but we could have called the variables any names we wanted to invent, as long as they were valid identifiers.

## Identifiers

A valid identifier is a sequence of one or more letters, digits or underscore characters (_). Neither spaces nor punctuation marks or symbols can be part of an identifier. Only letters, digits and single underscore characters are valid. In addition, variable identifiers always have to begin with a letter. They can also begin with an underline character (_ ), but in some cases these may be reserved for compiler specific keywords or external identifiers, as well as identifiers containing two successive underscore characters anywhere. In no case they can begin with a digit. Another rule that you have to consider when inventing your own identifiers is that they cannot match any keyword of the C++ language nor your compiler's specific ones, which are reserved keywords.

*The standard reserved keywords are*:

```
asm, auto, bool, break, case, catch, char,
class, const, const_cast, continue, default,
delete, do, double, dynamic_cast, else,
enum, explicit, export, extern, false,
float, for, friend, goto, if, inline, int,
long, mutable, namespace, new, operator,
private, protected, public, register,
reinterpret_cast, return, short, signed,
sizeof, static, static_cast, struct, switch,
template, this, throw, true, try, typedef,
typeid, typename, union, unsigned, using,
virtual, void, volatile, wchar_t, while
```

Additionally, alternative representations for some operators cannot be used as identifiers since they are reserved words under some circumstances:

```
and, and_eq, bitand, bitor, compl, not,
   not_eq, or, or_eq, xor, xor_eq
```

Your compiler may also include some additional specific reserved keywords.

*Very important*: The C++ language is a "case sensitive" language. That means that an identifier written in capital letters is not equivalent to another one with the same name but written in small letters. Thus, for example, the RESULT variable is not the same as the result variable or the Result variable. These are three different variable identifiers.

## Fundamental Data Types

When programming, we store the variables in our computer's memory, but the computer has to know what kind of data we want to store in them, since it is not going to occupy the same amount of memory to store a simple number than to store a single letter or a large number, and they are not going to be interpreted the same way. The memory in our computers is organized in bytes. A byte is the minimum amount of memory that we can manage in C++. A byte can store a relatively small amount of data: one single character or a small integer (generally an integer between 0 and 255). In addition, the computer can manipulate more complex data types that come from grouping several bytes, such as long numbers or non-integer numbers. Next you have a summary of the basic fundamental data types in C++, as well as the range of values that can be represented with each one:

| Name | Description | Size* | Range* |
|---|---|---|---|
| char | Character or small integer. | 1byte | signed: –128 to 127<br>unsigned: 0 to 255 |
| short int (short) | Short Integer. | 2bytes | signed: –32768 to 32767 unsigned: 0 to 65535 |
| int | Integer. | 4bytes | signed: - 2147483648 to 2147483647 unsigned: 0 to |

| | | | |
|---|---|---|---|
| | | | 4294967295 |
| long int (long) | Long integer. | 4bytes | signed: - 2147483648 to 2147483647 unsigned: 0 to 4294967295 |
| bool | Boolean value. It can take one of two values: true or false. | 1byte | true or false |
| float | Floating point number. | 4bytes | 3.4e +/– 38 (7 digits) |
| double | Double precision floating point number. | 8bytes | 1.7e +/– 308 (15 digits) |
| long double | Long double precision floating point number. | 8bytes | 1.7e +/– 308 (15 digits) |
| wchar_t | Wide character. | 2bytes | 1 wide character |

* The values of the columns Size and Range depend on the system the programme is compiled for. The values shown above are those found on most 32-bit systems.

But for other systems, the general specification is that int has the natural size suggested by the system architecture (one "*word*") and the four integer types char, short, int and long must each one be at least as large as the one preceding it, with char being always 1 byte in size.

The same applies to the floating point types float, double and long double, where each one must provide at least as much precision as the preceding one.

## Declaration of Variables

In order to use a variable in C++, we must first declare it specifying which data type we want it to be. The syntax to declare a new variable is to write the specifier of the desired data type (like int, bool, float...) followed by a valid variable identifier.

*For example*:

```
int a;b
float mynumber;
```

These are two valid declarations of variables. The first one declares a variable of type int with the identifier a. The second one declares a variable of type float with the identifier mynumber. Once declared, the variables a and mynumber can be used within the rest of their scope in the programme.

If you are going to declare more than one variable of the same type, you can declare all of them in a single statement by separating their identifiers with commas. For example:

```
int a, b, c;
```

This declares three variables (a, b and c), all of them of type int, and has exactly the same meaning as:

```
int a;
int b;
int c;
```

The integer data types char, short, long and int can be either signed or unsigned depending on the range of numbers needed to be represented. Signed types can represent both positive and negative values, whereas unsigned types can only represent positive values (and zero). This can be specified by using either the specifier signed or the specifier unsigned before the type name. For example:

```
unsigned short int NumberOfSisters;
signed int MyAccountBalance;
```

By default, if we do not specify either signed or unsigned most compiler settings will assume the type to be signed, therefore instead of the second declaration above we could have written:

```
int MyAccountBalance;
```

with exactly the same meaning (with or without the keyword signed) An exception to this general rule is the char type, which exists by itself and is considered a different fundamental data type from signed char and unsigned char, thought to store characters.

You should use either signed or unsigned if you intend to store numerical values in a char-sized variable. short and long can be used alone as type specifiers. In this case, they refer to their respective integer fundamental types: short is equivalent to short int and long is equivalent to long int. The following two variable declarations are equivalent:

```
short Year;
short int Year;
```

Finally, signed and unsigned may also be used as standalone type specifiers, meaning the same as signed int and unsigned int respectively. The following two declarations are equivalent:

```
unsigned NextYear;
unsigned int NextYear;
```

To see what variable declarations look like in action within a programme, we are going to see the C++ code of the example about your mental memory proposed at the beginning of this section:

```
// operating with variables
#include <iostream>
using namespace std;
int main ()
{
    // declaring variables:
    int a, b;
    int result;
    // process:
    a = 5;
    b = 2;
    a = a + 1;
    result = a - b;
    // print out the result:
    cout << result;
    // terminate the programme:
    return 0;
} 4
```

## Scope of Variables

All the variables that we intend to use in a programme must have been declared with its type specifier in an earlier point in the code, like we did in the previous code at the beginning of the body of the function main when we declared that a, b, and result were of type int.

A variable can be either of global or local scope. A global variable is a variable declared in the main body of the source code, outside all functions, while a local variable is one declared within the body of a function or a block.

```
#Include <iostream>
using namespace std;

int Integer;
char aCharacter;
char string [20];
unsigned int NumberOfSons;          ——— Global vabialbles

int main()
{

unsigned short Age;
float Anumber, AnotherOne;          ——— Local variables

count << "Enter your age:"
cin >> Age;
...                                 ——— Instructions
}
```

Global variables can be referred from anywhere in the code, even inside functions, whenever it is after its declaration.

The scope of local variables is limited to the block enclosed in braces ({}) where they are declared. For example, if they are declared at the beginning of the body of a function (like in function main) their scope is between its declaration point and the end of that function. In the example above, this means that if another function existed in addition to main, the local variables declared in main could not be accessed from the other function and vice versa.

## Initialization of Variables

When declaring a regular local variable, its value is by default undetermined. But you may want a variable to store a concrete value at the same moment that it is declared. In order to do that, you can initialize the variable. There are two ways to do this in C++: The first one, known as c-like, is done by appending an equal sign followed by the value to which the variable will be initialized:

```
type identifier = initial_value ;
```

For example, if we want to declare an int variable called a initialized with a value of 0 at the moment in which it is declared, we could write:

```
int a = 0;
```

The other way to initialize variables, known as constructor initialization, is done by enclosing the initial value between parentheses (()):

```
type identifier (initial_value) ;
```

```
For example:
int a (0);
Both ways of initializing variables are valid
    and equivalent in C++.
// initialization of variables
#include <iostream>
using namespace std;
int main ()
{
    int a=5; // initial value = 5
    int b(2); // initial value = 2
    int result; // initial value undetermined
    a = a + 3;
    result = a - b;
    cout << result;
    return 0;
} 6
```

## INTRODUCTION TO STRINGS

Variables that can store non-numerical values that are longer than one single character are known as strings.

The C++ language library provides support for strings through the standard string class. This is not a fundamental type, but it behaves in a similar way as fundamental types do in its most basic usage. A first difference with fundamental data types is that in order to declare and use objects (variables) of this type we need to include an additional header file in our source code: <string> and have access to the std namespace (which we already had in all our previous programmes thanks to the using namespace statement).

```
// my first string
    #include <iostream>
    #include <string>
    using namespace std;
    int main ()
{
 string mystring = "This is a string";
 cout << mystring;
```

```
 return 0;
}
```

output

```
This is a string
```

As you may see in the previous example, strings can be initialized with any valid string literal just like numerical type variables can be initialized to any valid numerical literal. Both initialization formats are valid with strings:

```
string mystring = "This is a string";
string mystring ("This is a string");
```

Strings can also perform all the other basic operations that fundamental data types can, like being declared without an initial value and being assigned values during execution:

```
// my first string
    #include <iostream>
    #include <string>
    using namespace std;
int main ()
{
    string mystring;
    mystring = "This is the initial string
    content";
    cout << mystring << endl;
    mystring = "This is a different string
    content";
    cout << mystring << endl;
    sreturn 0;
}
```

output

```
    This is the initial string content
    This is a different string content
```

For more details on C++ strings, you can have a look at the string class reference.

*Constants*: Constants are expressions with a fixed value.

## Literals

Literals are used to express particular values within the source code of a programme. We have already used these previously to give concrete values to variables or to express messages we wanted our programmes to print out, for example, when we wrote:

```
a = 5;
```

the 5 in this piece of code was a literal constant.

Literal constants can be divided in Integer Numerals, Floating-Point Numerals, Characters, Strings and Boolean Values.

## Integer Numerals

```
1776
707
-273
```

They are numerical constants that identify integer decimal values. Notice that to express a numerical constant we do not have to write quotes (") nor any special character. There is no doubt that it is a constant: whenever we write 1776 in a programme, we will be referring to the value 1776.

In addition to decimal numbers (those that all of us are used to use every day) C++ allows the use as literal constants of octal numbers (base 8) and hexadecimal numbers (base 16). If we want to express an octal number we have to precede it with a 0 (zero character). And in order to express a hexadecimal number we have to precede it with the characters 0x (zero, x). For example, the following literal constants are all equivalent to each other:

```
75      // decimal
0113     // octal
0x4b     // hexadecimal
```

All of these represent the same number: 75 (seventy-five) expressed as a base-10 numeral, octal numeral and hexadecimal numeral, respectively.

Literal constants, like variables, are considered to have a specific data type. By default, integer literals are of type int. However, we can force them to either be unsigned by appending the u character to it, or long by appending l:

```
75      // int
75u     // unsigned int
75l     // long
```

```
75ul     // unsigned long
```

In both cases, the suffix can be specified using either upper or lowercase letters.

## Floating Point Numbers

They express numbers with decimals and/or exponents. They can include either a decimal point, an e character (that expresses "by ten at the Xth height", where X is an integer value that follows the e character), or both a decimal point and an e character:

```
3.14159   // 3.14159
6.02e23   // 6.02 x 10^23
1.6e-19   // 1.6 x 10-19
3.0     // 3.0
```

These are four valid numbers with decimals expressed in C++. The first number is PI, the second one is the number of Avogadro, the third is the electric charge of an electron (an extremely small number) -all of them approximated- and the last one is the number three expressed as a floating-point numeric literal. The default type for floating point literals is double. If you explicitly want to express a float or long double numerical literal, you can use the f or l suffixes respectively:

```
3.14159L   // long double
6.02e23f   // float
```

Any of the letters than can be part of a floating-point numerical constant (e, f, l) can be written using either lower or uppercase letters without any difference in their meanings.

Character and string literals

There also exist non-numerical constants, like:

```
'z'
'p'
"Hello world"
"How do you do?"
```

The first two expressions represent single character constants, and the following two represent string literals composed of several characters. Notice that to represent a single character we enclose it between single quotes (') and to express a string (which generally consists of more than one character) we enclose it between double quotes ("). When writing both single character and string literals, it is necessary to put the quotation marks surrounding them to distinguish them from possible variable identifiers or reserved keywords. Notice the difference between these two expressions:

```
x
'x'
```

x alone would refer to a variable whose identifier is x, whereas 'x' (enclosed within single quotation marks) would refer to the character constant 'x'. Character and string literals have certain peculiarities, like the escape codes. These are special characters that are difficult or impossible to express otherwise in the source code of a programme, like newline (\n) or tab (\t). All of them are preceded by a backslash (\). Here you have a list of some of such escape codes:

```
\n newline
\r carriage return
\t tab
\v vertical tab
\b backspace
\f form feed (page feed)
\a alert (beep)
\' single quote (')
\" double quote (")
\? question mark (?)
\\ backslash (\)
For example:
'\n'
'\t'
"Left \t Right"
"one\ntwo\nthree"
```

Additionally, you can express any character by its numerical ASCII code by writing a backslash character (\) followed by the ASCII code expressed as an octal (base-8) or hexadecimal (base-16) number. In the first case (octal) the digits must immediately follow the backslash (for example \23 or \40), in the second case (hexadecimal), an x character must be written before the digits themselves (for example \x20 or \x4A). String literals can extend to more than a single line of code by putting a backslash sign (\) at the end of each unfinished line.

```
"string expressed in \
two lines"
```

You can also concatenate several string constants separating them by one or several blank spaces, tabulators, newline or any other valid blank character:

```
"this forms" "a single" "string" "of characters"
```

Finally, if we want the string literal to be explicitly made of wide characters (wchar_t), instead of narrow characters (char), we can precede the constant with the L prefix:

```
L"This is a wide character string"
```

Wide characters are used mainly to represent non-English or exotic character sets.

## BOOLEAN LITERALS

There are only two valid Boolean values: true and false. These can be expressed in C++ as values of type bool by using the Boolean literals true and false.

### Defined Constants (#define)

You can define your own names for constants that you use very often without having to resort to memory-consuming variables, simply by using the #define preprocessor directive. Its format is:

```
#define identifier value
For example:
#define PI 3.14159265
#define NEWLINE '\n'
```

This defines two new constants: PI and NEWLINE. Once they are defined, you can use them in the rest of the code as if they were any other regular constant, for example:

```
// defined constants: calculate circumference
#include <iostream>
using namespace std;
#define PI 3.14159
#define NEWLINE '\n'
int main ()
```

```
{
    double r=5.0;              // radius
    double circle;
    circle = 2 * PI * r;
    cout << circle;
    cout << NEWLINE;
    return 0;
}
output
31.4159
```

In fact the only thing that the compiler preprocessor does when it encounters #define directives is to literally replace any occurrence of their identifier (in the previous example, these were PI and NEWLINE) by the code to which they have been defined (3.14159265 and '\n' respectively). The #define directive is not a C++ statement but a directive for the preprocessor; therefore it assumes the entire line as the directive and does not require a semicolon (;) at its end. If you append a semicolon character (;) at the end, it will also be appended in all occurrences within the body of the programme that the preprocessor replaces.

## DECLARED CONSTANTS (CONST)

With the const prefix you can declare constants with a specific type in the same way as you would do with a variable:

```
const int pathwidth = 100;
const char tabulator = '\t';
```

Here, pathwidth and tabulator are two typed constants. They are treated just like regular variables except that their values cannot be modified after their definition.

## OPERATORS

Once we know of the existence of variables and constants, we can begin to operate with them. For that purpose, C++ integrates operators. Unlike other languages whose operators are mainly keywords, operators in C++ are mostly made of signs that are not part of the alphabet but are available in all keyboards. This makes C++ code shorter and more international, since it relies less on English words, but requires a little of learning effort in the beginning.

You do not have to memorize all the content of this page. Most details are only provided to serve as a later reference in case you need it.

## ASSIGNMENT (=)

The assignment operator assigns a value to a variable.

```
a = 5;
```

This statement assigns the integer value 5 to the variable a. The part at the left of the assignment operator (=) is known as the *lvalue* (left value) and the right one as the *rvalue* (right value). The lvalue has to be a variable whereas the rvalue can be either a constant, a variable, the result of an operation or any combination of these. The most important rule when assigning is the *right-to-left* rule: The assignment operation always takes place from right to left, and never the other way:

```
a = b;
```

This statement assigns to variable a (the lvalue) the value contained in variable b (the rvalue). The value that was stored until this moment in a is not considered at all in this operation, and in fact that value is lost. Consider also that we are only assigning the value of b to a at the moment of the assignment operation. Therefore a later change of b will not affect the new value of a.

For example, let us have a look at the following code - I have included the evolution of the content stored in the variables as comments:

```
// assignment operator
#include <iostream>
using namespace std;
int main ()
{
    int a, b;         // a:?, b:?
    a = 10;          // a:10, b:?
    b = 4;          // a:10, b:4
    a = b;          // a:4, b:4
    b = 7;          // a:4, b:7
    cout << "a:";
```

```
    cout << a;
    cout << " b:";
    cout << b;
    return 0;
}
output
a:4 b:7
```

This code will give us as result that the value contained in a is 4 and the one contained in b is 7. Notice how a was not affected by the final modification of b, even though we declared a = b earlier (that is because of the *right-to-left rule*).

A property that C++ has over other programming languages is that the assignment operation can be used as the rvalue (or part of an rvalue) for another assignment operation. For example:

```
a = 2 + (b = 5);
```

is equivalent to:

```
b = 5;
a = 2 + b;
```

that means: first assign 5 to variable b and then assign to a the value 2 plus the result of the previous assignment of b (*i.e.* 5), leaving a with a final value of 7. The following expression is also valid in C++,

```
a = b = c = 5;
```

It assigns 5 to the all the three variables: a, b and c.

Arithmetic operators ( +, -, *, /, % )

The five arithmetical operations supported by the C++ language are:

```
+ addition
- subtraction
* multiplication
/ division
% modulo
```

Operations of addition, subtraction, multiplication and division literally correspond with their respective mathematical operators.

The only one that you might not be so used to see may be *modulo*; whose operator is the percentage sign (%). Modulo is the operation that gives the remainder of a division of two values. For example, if we write:

```
a = 11 % 3;
```

the variable a will contain the value 2, since 2 is the remainder from dividing 11 between 3.

**Compound assignment (+=, -=, *=, /=, %=, >>=, <<=, &=, ^=, |=)**

When we want to modify the value of a variable by performing an operation on the value currently stored in that variable we can use compound assignment operators:

| expression | is equivalent to |
|---|---|
| `value += increase;` | `value = value + increase;` |
| `a -= 5;` | `a = a - 5;` |
| `a /= b;` | `a = a / b;` |
| `price *= units + 1;` | `price = price * (units + 1);` |

and the same for all other operators. For example:

```
// compound assignment operators
#include <iostream>
using namespace std;
int main ()
{
    int a, b=3;
    a = b;
    a+=2;          // equivalent to a=a+2
    cout << a;
    return 0;
} 5
```

**Increase and decrease (++, —)**

Shortening even more some expressions, the increase operator (++) and the decrease operator (—) increase or reduce by one the value stored in a variable. They are equivalent to +=1 and to -=1, respectively.

*Thus:*

```
c++;
c+=1;
c=c+1;
```

are all equivalent in its functionality: the three of them increase by one the value of c.In the early C compilers, the three previous expressions probably produced different executable code depending on which one was used. Nowadays, this type of code optimization is generally done automatically by the compiler, thus the three expressions should produce exactly the same executable code.

A characteristic of this operator is that it can be used both as a prefix and as a suffix. That means that it can be written either before the variable identifier (++a) or after it (a++). Although in simple expressions like a++ or ++a both have exactly the same meaning, in other expressions in which the result of the increase or decrease operation is evaluated as a value in an outer expression they may have an important difference in their meaning: In the case that the increase operator is used as a prefix (++a) the value is increased before the result of the expression is evaluated and therefore the increased value is considered in the outer expression; in case that it is used as a suffix (a++) the value stored in a is increased after being evaluated and therefore the value stored before the increase operation is evaluated in the outer expression.

*Notice the difference*:

| Example 1 | Example 2 |
|---|---|
| B=3; | B=3; |
| A=++B; | A=B++; |
| // A contains 4, B contains 4 | // A contains 3, B contains 4s |

In Example 1, B is increased before its value is copied to A. While in Example 2, the value of B is copied to A and then B is increased.

### Relational and Equality Operators ( ==, !=, >, <, >=, <= )

In order to evaluate a comparison between two expressions we can use the relational and equality operators. The result of a relational operation is a Boolean value that can only be true or false, according to its Boolean result.We may want to compare two expressions, for example, to know if they are equal or if one is greater than the other is. Here is a list of the relational and equality operators that can be used in C++:

```
==  Equal to
!=  Not equal to
```

```
>   Greater than
<   Less than
>=  Greater than or equal to
<=  Less than or equal to
```

Here there are some examples:

```
(7 == 5)   // evaluates to false.
(5 > 4)   // evaluates to true.
(3 != 2)   // evaluates to true.
(6 >= 6)   // evaluates to true.
(5 < 5)   // evaluates to false.
```

Of course, instead of using only numeric constants, we can use any valid expression, including variables. Suppose that a=2, b=3 and c=6,

```
(a == 5)   // evaluates to false since a is not
    equal to 5.
(a*b >= c)  // evaluates to true since (2*3 >=
    6) is true.
(b+4 > a*c) // evaluates to false since (3+4 >
    2*6) is false.
((b=2) == a) // evaluates to true.
```

Be careful! The operator = (one equal sign) is not the same as the operator == (two equal signs), the first one is an assignment operator (assigns the value at its right to the variable at its left) and the other one (==) is the equality operator that compares whether both expressions in the two sides of it are equal to each other. Thus, in the last expression ((b=2) == a), we first assigned the value 2 to b and then we compared it to a, that also stores the value 2, so the result of the operation is true.

**Logical operators ( !, &&, || )**

The Operator ! is the C++ operator to perform the Boolean operation NOT, it has only one operand, located at its right, and the only thing that it does is to inverse the value of it, producing false if its operand is true and true if its operand is false. Basically, it returns the opposite Boolean value of evaluating its operand. For example:

```
!(5 == 5)   // evaluates to false because the
    expression at its right (5 == 5) is true.
```

```
!(6 <= 4)   // evaluates to true because (6 <=
    4) would be false.
!true     // evaluates to false
!false     // evaluates to true.
```

The logical operators && and || are used when evaluating two expressions to obtain a single relational result. The operator && corresponds with Boolean logical operation AND. This operation results true if both its two operands are true, and false otherwise. The following panel shows the result of operator && evaluating the expression a && b:

**&& OPERATOR**

| a | b | a && b |
|---|---|---|
| true | true | true |
| true | false | false |
| false | true | false |
| false | false | false |

The operator || corresponds with Boolean logical operation OR. This operation results true if either one of its two operands is true, thus being false only when both operands are false themselves. Here are the possible results of a || b:

**|| OPERATOR**

| a | b | a \|\| b |
|---|---|---|
| true | true | true |
| true | false | true |
| false | true | true |
| false | false | false |

*For example:*

```
( (5 == 5) && (3 > 6) ) // evaluates to false (
    true && false ).
( (5 == 5) || (3 > 6) ) // evaluates to true (
    true || false ).
```

**Conditional operator ( ? )**

The conditional operator evaluates an expression returning a value if that expression is true and a different one if the expression is evaluated as false. Its format is:

```
condition ? result1: result2
```

If condition is true the expression will return result1, if it is not it will return result2.

```
7==5 ? 4 : 3    // returns 3, since 7 is not
    equal to 5.
7==5+2 ? 4 : 3  // returns 4, since 7 is equal
    to 5+2.
5>3 ? a : b   // returns the value of a, since
    5 is greater than 3.
a>b ? a : b   // returns whichever is greater,
    a or b.

// conditional operator

#include <iostream>
using namespace std;

int main ()
{
 int a,b,c;

 a=2;
 b=7;
 c = (a>b) ? a : b;

 cout << c;

 return 0;
} 7
```

In this example a was 2 and b was 7, so the expression being evaluated (a>b) was not true, thus the first value specified after the question mark was discarded in favour of the second value (the one after the colon) which was b, with a value of 7.

### Comma Operator ( , )

The comma operator (,) is used to separate two or more expressions that are included where only one expression is expected. When the set of expressions has to be evaluated for a value, only the rightmost expression is considered.

*For example, the following code*:

```
a = (b=3, b+2);
```

Would first assign the value 3 to b, and then assign b+2 to variable a. So, at the end, variable a would contain the value 5 while variable b would contain value 3.

## Bitwise Operators ( &, |, ^, ~, <<, >> )

Bitwise operators modify variables considering the bit patterns that represent the values they store.

| Operator | Asm equivalent | Description |
|---|---|---|
| & | AND | Bitwise AND |
| \| | OR | Bitwise Inclusive OR |
| ^ | XOR | Bitwise Exclusive OR |
| ~ | NOT | Unary complement (bit inversion) |
| << | SHL | Shift Left |
| >> | SHR | Shift Right |

## Explicit type Casting Operator

Type casting operators allow you to convert a datum of a given type to another. There are several ways to do this in C++. The simplest one, which has been inherited from the C language, is to precede the expression to be converted by the new type enclosed between parentheses (()):

```
int i;
float f = 3.14;
i = (int) f;
```

The previous code converts the float number 3.14 to an integer value (3), the remainder is lost. Here, the typecasting operator was (int). Another way to do the same thing in C++ is using the functional notation: preceding the expression to be converted by the type and enclosing the expression between parentheses:

```
i = int ( f );
```

Both ways of type casting are valid in C++.

## Sizeof()

This operator accepts one parameter, which can be either a type or a variable itself and returns the size in bytes of that type or object:

```
a = sizeof (char);
```

This will assign the value 1 to a because char is a one-byte long type. The value returned by sizeof is a constant, so it is always determined before programme execution.

## Other Operators

Later in these tutorials, we will see a few more operators, like the ones referring to pointers or the specifics for object-oriented programming. Each one is treated in its respective section.

## Precedence of Operators

When writing complex expressions with several operands, we may have some doubts about which operand is evaluated first and which later. For example, in this expression:

```
a = 5 + 7 % 2
```

we may doubt if it really means:

```
a = 5 + (7 % 2)   // with a result of 6, or
a = (5 + 7) % 2   // with a result of 0
```

The correct answer is the first of the two expressions, with a result of 6. There is an established order with the priority of each operator, and not only the arithmetic ones (those whose preference come from mathematics) but for all the operators which can appear in C++. From greatest to lowest priority, the priority order is as follows:

| Level | Operator | Description | Grouping |
|---|---|---|---|
| 1 | :: | scope | Left-to-right |
| 2 | () [] . -> ++ — dynamic_cast static_cast reinterpret_cast const_cast typeid | postfix | Left-to-right |
| 3 | ++ — ~ !sizeof new delete | unary (prefix) | Right-to-left |
| | * & | indirection and reference (pointers) | Right-to-left |
| | + - | unary sign operator | |
| 4 | (type) | type casting | Right-to-left |
| 5 | .* ->* | pointer-to-member | Left-to-right |
| 6 | * / % | multiplicative | Left-to-right |
| 7 | + - | additive | Left-to-right |
| 8 | << >> | shift | Left-to-right |
| 9 | < > <= >= | relational | Left-to-right |

<table>
<tr><td>10</td><td>== !=</td><td>equality</td><td>Left-to-right</td></tr>
<tr><td>11</td><td>&</td><td>bitwise AND</td><td>Left-to-right</td></tr>
<tr><td>12</td><td>^</td><td>bitwise XOR</td><td>Left-to-right</td></tr>
<tr><td>13</td><td>|</td><td>bitwise OR</td><td>Left-to-right</td></tr>
<tr><td>14</td><td>&&</td><td>logical AND</td><td>Left-to-right</td></tr>
<tr><td>15</td><td>||</td><td>logical OR</td><td>Left-to-right</td></tr>
<tr><td>16</td><td>?:</td><td>conditional</td><td>Right-to-left</td></tr>
<tr><td>17</td><td>= *= /= %= += -= >>=<br><<= &= ^= |=</td><td>assignment</td><td>Right-to-left</td></tr>
<tr><td>18</td><td>,</td><td>comma</td><td>Left-to-right</td></tr>
</table>

Grouping defines the precedence order in which operators are evaluated in the case that there are several operators of the same level in an expression.

All these precedence levels for operators can be manipulated or become more legible by removing possible ambiguities using parentheses signs ( and ), as in this example:

```
a = 5 + 7 % 2;
```

might be written either as:

```
a = 5 + (7 % 2);
or
a = (5 + 7) % 2;
```

depending on the operation that we want to perform.

So if you want to write complicated expressions and you are not completely sure of the precedence levels, always include parentheses. It will also become a code easier to read.

## Basic Input/Output

Until now, the example programmes of previous sections provided very little interaction with the user, if any at all. Using the standard input and output library, we will be able to interact with the user by printing messages on the screen and getting the user's input from the keyboard. C++ uses a convenient abstraction called *streams* to perform input and output operations in sequential media such as the screen or the keyboard. A stream is an object where a programme can either insert or extract characters to/from it. We do not really need to care about many specifications about the physical media associated with the stream - we only need to know it will accept or provide characters sequentialy. The standard C++ library includes the header file iostream, where the standard input and output stream objects are declared.

**Standard Output (cout)**

By default, the standard output of a programme is the screen, and the C++ stream object defined to access it is cout.

cout is used in conjunction with the *insertion operator,* which is written as << (two "less than" signs).

```
cout << "Output sentence"; // prints Output
    sentence on screen
cout << 120; / prints number 120 on screen
cout << x; // prints the content of x on screen
```

The << operator inserts the data that follows it into the stream preceding it. In the examples above it inserted the constant string Output sentence, the numerical constant 120 and variable x into the standard output stream cout. Notice that the sentence in the first instruction is enclosed between double quotes (") because it is a constant string of characters. Whenever we want to use constant strings of characters we must enclose them between double quotes (") so that they can be clearly distinguished from variable names. For example, these two sentences have very different results:

```
cout << "Hello"; // prints Hello
cout << Hello;  // prints the content of Hello
    variable
```

The insertion operator (<<) may be used more than once in a single statement:

```
cout << "Hello, " << "I am " << "a C++ statement";
```

This last statement would print the message Hello, I am a C++ statement on the screen. The utility of repeating the insertion operator (<<) is demonstrated when we want to print out a combination of variables and constants or more than one variable:

```
cout << "Hello, I am " << age << " years old and
    my zipcode is " << zipcode;
```

If we assume the age variable to contain the value 24 and the zipcode variable to contain 90064 the output of the previous statement would be:

```
Hello, I am 24 years old and my zipcode is
    90064
```

It is important to notice that cout does not add a line break after its output unless we explicitly indicate it, therefore, the following statements:

```
cout << "This is a sentence.";
cout << "This is another sentence.";
```

will be shown on the screen one following the other without any line break between them:

This is a sentence.This is another sentence.

even though we had written them in two different insertions into cout. In order to perform a line break on the output we must explicitly insert a new-line character into cout. In C++ a new-line character can be specified as \n (backslash, n):

```
cout << "First sentence.\n ";
cout << "Second sentence.\nThird sentence.";
This produces the following output:
First sentence.
Second sentence.
```

Third sentence.

Additionally, to add a new-line, you may also use the endl manipulator. For example:

```
cout << "First sentence." << endl;
cout << "Second sentence." << endl;
would print out:
First sentence.
Second sentence.
```

The endl manipulator produces a newline character, exactly as the insertion of '\n' does, but it also has an additional behaviour when it is used with buffered streams: the buffer is flushed.

Anyway, cout will be an unbuffered stream in most cases, so you can generally use both the \n escape character and the endl manipulator in order to specify a new line without any difference in its behaviour.

## Standard Input (cin)

The standard input device is usually the keyboard.

Handling the standard input in C++ is done by applying the overloaded operator of extraction (>>) on the cin stream. The operator must be followed by the variable that will store the data that is going to be extracted from the stream. For example:

```
int age;
cin >> age;
```

The first statement declares a variable of type int called age, and the second one waits for an input from cin (the keyboard) in order to store it in this integer variable.

cin can only process the input from the keyboard once the RETURN key has been pressed. Therefore, even if you request a single character, the extraction from cin will not process the input until the user presses RETURN after the character has been introduced. You must always consider the type of the variable that you are using as a container with cin extractions. If you request an integer you will get an integer, if you request a character you will get a character and if you request a string of characters you will get a string of characters.

```
// i/o example
#include <iostream>
using namespace std;
int main ()
{
    int i;
    cout << "Please enter an integer value: ";
    cin >> i;
    cout << "The value you entered is " << i;
    cout << " and its double is " << i*2 <<
    ".\n";
    return 0;
} Please enter an integer value: 702
The value you entered is 702 and its double is
    1404.
```

The user of a programme may be one of the factors that generate errors even in the simplest programmes that use cin (like the one we have just seen). Since if you request an integer value and the user introduces a name (which generally is a string of characters), the result may cause your programme to misoperate since it is not what we were expecting from the user. So when you use the data input provided by cin extractions you will have to trust that the user of your programme will be cooperative and that he/she will not introduce his/her name or something similar when an integer value is requested.

A little ahead, when we see the stringstream class we will see a possible solution for the errors that can be caused by this type of user input.

*You can also use cin to request more than one datum input from the user:*

```
cin >> a >> b;
```

*is equivalent to:*

```
cin >> a;
cin >> b;
```

In both cases the user must give two data, one for variable a and another one for variable b that may be separated by any valid blank separator: a space, a tab character or a newline.

## Cin and Strings

We can use cin to get strings with the extraction operator (>>) as we do with fundamental data type variables:

```
cin >> mystring;
```

However, as it has been said, cin extraction stops reading as soon as if finds any blank space character, so in this case we will be able to get just one word for each extraction.

This behaviour may or may not be what we want; for example if we want to get a sentence from the user, this extraction operation would not be useful.

In order to get entire lines, we can use the function getline, which is the more recommendable way to get user input with cin:

```
// cin with strings
#include <iostream>
#include <string>
using namespace std;

int main ()
```

```
{
    string mystr;
    cout << "What's your name? ";
    getline (cin, mystr);
    cout << "Hello " << mystr << ".\n";
    cout << "What is your favourite team? ";
    getline (cin, mystr);
    cout << "I like " << mystr << " too!\n";
    return 0;
} What's your name? Juan Soulié
Hello Juan Soulié.
What is your favourite team? The Isotopes
I like The Isotopes too!
```

Notice how in both calls to getline we used the same string identifier (mystr). What the programme does in the second call is simply to replace the previous content by the new one that is introduced.

## Stringstream

The standard header file <sstream> defines a class called stringstream that allows a string-based object to be treated as a stream. This way we can perform extraction or insertion operations from/to strings, which is especially useful to convert strings to numerical values and vice versa. For example, if we want to extract an integer from a string we can write:

```
string mystr ("1204");
int myint;
stringstream(mystr) >> myint;
```

This declares a string object with a value of "1204", and an int object. Then we use stringstream's constructor to construct an object of this type from the string object. Because we can use stringstream objects as if they were streams, we can extract an integer from it as we would have done on cin by applying the extractor operator (>>) on it followed by a variable of type int.

After this piece of code, the variable myint will contain the numerical value 1204.

```
// stringstreams
#include <iostream>
#include <string>
#include <sstream>
using namespace std;
int main ()
{
 string mystr;
 float price=0;
 int quantity=0;
 cout << "Enter price: ";
 getline (cin,mystr);
 stringstream(mystr) >> price;
 cout << "Enter quantity: ";
 getline (cin,mystr);
 stringstream(mystr) >> quantity;
 cout << "Total price: " << price*quantity <<
   endl;
 return 0;
} Enter price: 22.25
Enter quantity: 7
Total price: 155.75
```

In this example, we acquire numeric values from the standard input indirectly. Instead of extracting numeric values directly from the standard input, we get lines from the standard input (cin) into a string object (mystr), and then we extract the integer values from this string into a variable of type int (myint). Using this method, instead of direct extractions of integer values, we have more control over what happens with the input of numeric values from the user, since we are separating the process of obtaining input from the user (we now simply ask for lines) with the interpretation of that input. Therefore, this method is usually preferred to get numerical values from the user in all programmes that are intensive in user input.

## Control Structures

A programme is usually not limited to a linear sequence

of instructions. During its process it may bifurcate, repeat code or take decisions. For that purpose, C++ provides control structures that serve to specify what has to be done by our programme, when and under which circumstances.

With the introduction of control structures we are going to have to introduce a new concept: the *compound-statement* or *block*. A block is a group of statements which are separated by semicolons (;) like all C++ statements, but grouped together in a block enclosed in braces: { }:

```
{ statement1; statement2; statement3; }
```

Most of the control structures that we will see in this section require a generic statement as part of its syntax. A statement can be either a simple statement (a simple instruction ending with a semicolon) or a compound statement (several instructions grouped in a block), like the one just described.

In the case that we want the statement to be a simple statement, we do not need to enclose it in braces ({}). But in the case that we want the statement to be a compound statement it must be enclosed between braces ({}), forming a block.

Conditional structure: if and else

The if keyword is used to execute a statement or block only if a condition is fulfilled. Its form is:

if (condition) statement

Where condition is the expression that is being evaluated. If this condition is true, statement is executed. If it is false, statement is ignored (not executed) and the programme continues right after this conditional structure.

For example, the following code fragment prints x is 100 only if the value stored in the x variable is indeed 100:

```
if (x == 100)
    cout << "x is 100";
```

If we want more than a single statement to be executed in case that the condition is true we can specify a block using braces { }:

```
if (x == 100)
{
    cout << "x is ";
```

```
    cout << x;
}
```

We can additionally specify what we want to happen if the condition is not fulfilled by using the keyword else. Its form used in conjunction with if is:

if (condition) statement1 else statement2

For example:

```
if (x == 100)
    cout << "x is 100";
else
    cout << "x is not 100";
```

prints on the screen x is 100 if indeed x has a value of 100, but if it has not -and only if not- it prints out x is not 100.

The if + else structures can be concatenated with the intention of verifying a range of values. The following example shows its use telling if the value currently stored in x is positive, negative or none of them (*i.e.* zero):

```
if (x > 0)
    cout << "x is positive";
else if (x < 0)
    cout << "x is negative";
else
    cout << "x is 0";
```

Remember that in case that we want more than a single statement to be executed, we must group them in a block by enclosing them in braces { }.

## ITERATION STRUCTURES (LOOPS)

Loops have as purpose to repeat a statement a certain number of times or while a condition is fulfilled.

### The While Loop

*Its format is:*

while (expression) statement

and its functionality is simply to repeat statement while the condition set in expression is true. For example, we are going to make a programme to countdown using a while-loop:

```
// custom countdown using while
```

```
#include <iostream>
using namespace std;
int main ()
{
    int n;
    cout << "Enter the starting number > ";
    cin >> n;
    while (n>0) {
    cout << n << ", ";
    —n;
}

  cout << "FIRE!\n";
  return 0;
}
Output
Enter the starting number > 8
8, 7, 6, 5, 4, 3, 2, 1, FIRE!
```

When the programme starts the user is prompted to insert a starting number for the countdown. Then the while loop begins, if the value entered by the user fulfills the condition n>0 (that n is greater than zero) the block that follows the condition will be executed and repeated while the condition (n>0) remains being true. The whole process of the previous programme can be interpreted according to the following script (beginning in main):

1. User assigns a value to n
2. The while condition is checked (n>0). At this point there are two posibilities:
   - Condition is true: statement is executed (to step 3)
   - Condition is false: ignore statement and continue after it (to step 5)
3. Execute statement:
   cout << n << ", "; —n;
   (prints the value of n on the screen and decreases n by 1)
4. End of block. Return automatically to step 2

5. Continue the programme right after the block: print FIRE! and end programme.

When creating a while-loop, we must always consider that it has to end at some point, therefore we must provide within the block some method to force the condition to become false at some point, otherwise the loop will continue looping forever. In this case we have included —n; that decreases the value of the variable that is being evaluated in the condition (n) by one - this will eventually make the condition (n>0) to become false after a certain number of loop iterations: to be more specific, when n becomes 0, that is where our while-loop and our countdown end.

Of course this is such a simple action for our computer that the whole countdown is performed instantly without any practical delay between numbers.

The do-while loop

Its format is:

do statement while (condition);

Its functionality is exactly the same as the while loop, except that condition in the do-while loop is evaluated after the execution of statement instead of before, granting at least one execution of statement even if condition is never fulfilled. For example, the following example programme echoes any number you enter until you enter 0.

```
// number echoer
#include <iostream>
using namespace std;
int main ()
{
    unsigned long n;
    do {
    cout << "Enter number (0 to end): ";
    cin >> n;
    cout << "You entered: " << n << "\n";
    } while (n != 0);
    return 0;
} Enter number (0 to end): 12345
You entered: 12345
```

```
output
Enter number (0 to end): 160277
You entered: 160277
Enter number (0 to end): 0
You entered: 0
```

The do-while loop is usually used when the condition that has to determine the end of the loop is determined within the loop statement itself, like in the previous case, where the user input within the block is what is used to determine if the loop has to end. In fact if you never enter the value 0 in the previous example you can be prompted for more numbers forever.

The for loop

Its format is: for (initialization; condition; increase) statement; and its main function is to repeat statement while condition remains true, like the while loop. But in addition, the for loop provides specific locations to contain an initialization statement and an increase statement. So this loop is specially designed to perform a repetitive action with a counter which is initialized and increased on each iteration.

*It works in the following way*:

1. *Initialization is executed*: Generally it is an initial value setting for a counter variable. This is executed only once.
2. *Condition is checked*: If it is true the loop continues, otherwise the loop ends and statement is skipped (not executed).
3. *Statement is executed*: As usual, it can be either a single statement or a block enclosed in braces { }.
4. Finally, whatever is specified in the increase field is executed and the loop gets back to step 2.

Here is an example of countdown using a for loop:

```
// countdown using a for loop
#include <iostream>
using namespace std;
int main ()
{
    for (int n=10; n>0; n–) {
    cout << n << ", ";
```

```
    }
    cout << "FIRE!\n";
    return 0;
}
```

**output**

**10, 9, 8, 7, 6, 5, 4, 3, 2, 1, FIRE!**

The initialization and increase fields are optional. They can remain empty, but in all cases the semicolon signs between them must be written. For example we could write: for (;n<10;) if we wanted to specify no initialization and no increase; or for (;n<10;n++) if we wanted to include an increase field but no initialization (maybe because the variable was already initialized before).Optionally, using the comma operator (,) we can specify more than one expression in any of the fields included in a for loop, like in initialization, for example. The comma operator (,) is an expression separator, it serves to separate more than one expression where only one is generally expected. For example, suppose that we wanted to initialize more than one variable in our loop:

```
for ( n=0, i=100 ; n!=i ; n++, i– )
{
    // whatever here...
}
```

This loop will execute for 50 times if neither n or i are modified within the loop:

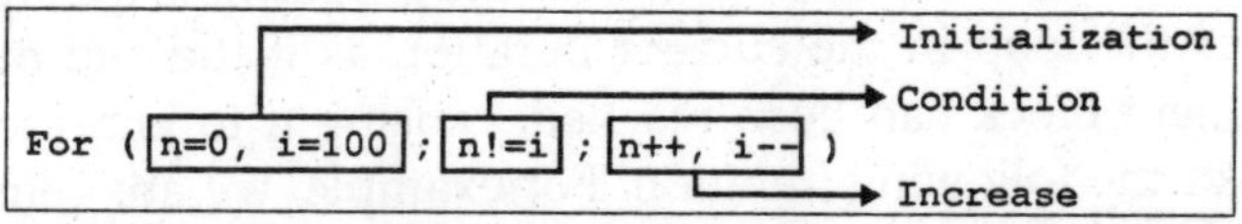


n starts with a value of 0, and i with 100, the condition is n!=i (that n is not equal to i). Because n is increased by one and i decreased by one, the loop's condition will become false after the 50th loop, when both n and i will be equal to 50.

## JUMP STATEMENTS

### The Break Statement

Using break we can leave a loop even if the condition for its end is not fulfilled. It can be used to end an infinite loop, or to force it to end before its natural end. For example, we are going to stop the count down before its natural end (maybe because of an engine check failure?):

```
// break loop example
#include <iostream>
using namespace std;
int main ()
{
    int n;
    for (n=10; n>0; n–)
    {
    cout << n << ", ";
    if (n==3)
    {
          cout << "countdown aborted!";
          break;
          }
    }
  return 0;
}
output
10, 9, 8, 7, 6, 5, 4, 3, countdown aborted!
```

### The Continue Statement

The continue statement causes the programme to skip the rest of the loop in the current iteration as if the end of the statement block had been reached, causing it to jump to the start of the following iteration. For example, we are going to skip the number 5 in our countdown:

```
// continue loop example
#include <iostream>
using namespace std;
int main ()
{
    for (int n=10; n>0; n–) {
          if (n==5) continue;
    cout << n << ", ";
    }
```

```
    cout << "FIRE!\n";
    return 0;
}
output
10, 9, 8, 7, 6, 4, 3, 2, 1, FIRE!
```

## The Goto Statement

Goto allows to make an absolute jump to another point in the programme. You should use this feature with caution since its execution causes an unconditional jump ignoring any type of nesting limitations.

The destination point is identified by a label, which is then used as an argument for the goto statement. A label is made of a valid identifier followed by a colon (:). Generally speaking, this instruction has no concrete use in structured or object oriented programming aside from those that low-level programming fans may find for it. For example, here is our countdown loop using goto:

```
// goto loop example
#include <iostream>
using namespace std;
int main ()
{
    int n=10;
    loop:
    cout << n << ", ";
    n—;
    if (n>0) goto loop;
    cout << "FIRE!\n";
    return 0;
}
output
10, 9, 8, 7, 6, 5, 4, 3, 2, 1, FIRE!
```

The exit function exit is a function defined in the cstdlib library.

*The purpose of exit is to terminate the current programme with a specific exit code. Its prototype is:*

```
void exit (int exitcode);
```

The exitcode is used by some operating systems and may be used by calling programmes. By convention, an exit code of 0 means that the programme finished normally and any other value means that some error or unexpected results happened.

The selective structure: switch.

The syntax of the switch statement is a bit peculiar. Its objective is to check several possible constant values for an expression. Something similar to what we did at the beginning of this section with the concatenation of several if and else if instructions. Its form is the following:

```
switch (expression)
{
    case constant1:
    group of statements 1;
    break;
    case constant2:
    group of statements 2;
    break;
    .
    .
    .
    default:
    default group of statements
}
```

It works in the following way: switch evaluates expression and checks if it is equivalent to constant1, if it is, it executes group of statements 1 until it finds the break statement. When it finds this break statement the programme jumps to the end of the switch selective structure.If expression was not equal to constant1 it will be checked against constant2. If it is equal to this, it will execute group of statements 2 until a break keyword is found, and then will jump to the end of the switch selective structure. Finally, if the value of expression did not match any of the previously specified constants (you can include as many case labels as values you want to check), the programme will execute the statements included after the default: label, if it exists (since it is optional).

Both of the following code fragments have the same behaviour: switch example if-else equivalent

```
switch (x) {
    case 1:
          cout << "x is 1";
          break;
    case 2:
          cout << "x is 2";
          break;
    default:
          cout << "value of x unknown";
    } if (x == 1) {
    cout << "x is 1";
    }
else if (x == 2) {
    cout << "x is 2";
    }
else {
    cout << "value of x unknown";
}
```

The switch statement is a bit peculiar within the C++ language because it uses labels instead of blocks. This forces us to put break statements after the group of statements that we want to be executed for a specific condition. Otherwise the remainder statements -including those corresponding to other labels- will also be executed until the end of the switch selective block or a break statement is reached.

For example, if we did not include a break statement after the first group for case one, the programme will not automatically jump to the end of the switch selective block and it would continue executing the rest of statements until it reaches either a break instruction or the end of the switch selective block. This makes unnecessary to include braces { } surrounding the statements for each of the cases, and it can also be useful to execute the same block of instructions for different possible values for the expression being evaluated. For example:

```
switch (x) {
    case 1:
```

```
    case 2:
    case 3:
         cout << "x is 1, 2 or 3";
    break;
    default:
    cout << "x is not 1, 2 nor 3";
}
```

Notice that switch can only be used to compare an expression against constants. Therefore we cannot put variables as labels (for example case n: where n is a variable) or ranges (case (1..3):) because they are not valid C++ constants.

If you need to check ranges or values that are not constants, use a concatenation of if and else if statements.

## FUNCTIONS (I)

Using functions we can structure our programmes in a more modular way, accessing all the potential that structured programming can offer to us in C++.A function is a group of statements that is executed when it is called from some point of the programme. The following is its format:

```
type name ( parameter1, parameter2, ...) {
statements }
```

*where*:

- Type is the data type specifier of the data returned by the function.
- Name is the identifier by which it will be possible to call the function.
- Parameters (as many as needed): Each parameter consists of a data type specifier followed by an identifier, like any regular variable declaration (for example: int x) and which acts within the function as a regular local variable. They allow to pass arguments to the function when it is called. The different parameters are separated by commas.
- Statements is the function's body. It is a block of statements surrounded by braces { }.

*Here you have the first function example*:

```
// function example
```

```
#include <iostream>
using namespace std;
int addition (int a, int b)
{
    int r;
    r=a+b;
    return (r);
}
int main ()
{
    int z;
    z = addition (5,3);
    cout << "The result is " << z;
    return 0;
} The result is 8
```

In order to examine this code, first of all remember something said at the beginning of this tutorial: a C++ programme always begins its execution by the main function. So we will begin there.

We can see how the main function begins by declaring the variable z of type int. Right after that, we see a call to a function called addition. Paying attention we will be able to see the similarity between the structure of the call to the function and the declaration of the function itself some code lines above:

```
Int addition (int a,  int b)
               ↑       ↑
               |       |
z = addition (5,       3);
```

The parameters and arguments have a clear correspondence. Within the main function we called to addition passing two values: 5 and 3, that correspond to the int a and int b parameters declared for function addition.

At the point at which the function is called from within main, the control is lost by main and passed to function addition. The value of both arguments passed in the call (5 and 3) are copied to the local variables int a and int b within the function.

Function addition declares another local variable (int r), and by means of the expression r=a+b, it assigns to r the result of a plus b. Because the actual parameters passed for a and b are 5 and 3 respectively, the result is 8.

*The following line of code*:

```
return (r);
```

finalizes function addition, and returns the control back to the function that called it in the first place (in this case, main). At this moment the programme follows it regular course from the same point at which it was interrupted by the call to addition. But additionally, because the return statement in function addition specified a value: the content of variable r (return (r);), which at that moment had a value of 8. This value becomes the value of evaluating the function call.

```
Int addition (int a, int b)
 8

z = addition (5,        3);
```

So being the value returned by a function the value given to the function call itself when it is evaluated, the variable z will be set to the value returned by addition (5, 3), that is 8. To explain it another way, you can imagine that the call to a function (addition (5,3)) is literally replaced by the value it returns (8).

*The following line of code in main is*:

```
cout << "The result is " << z;
```

That, as you may already expect, produces the printing of the result on the screen.

## Scope of Variables

The scope of variables declared within a function or any other inner block is only their own function or their own block and cannot be used outside of them. For example, in the previous example it would have been impossible to use the variables a, b or r directly in function main since they were variables local to function addition. Also, it would have been impossible to use the variable z directly within function addition, since this was a variable local to the function main.

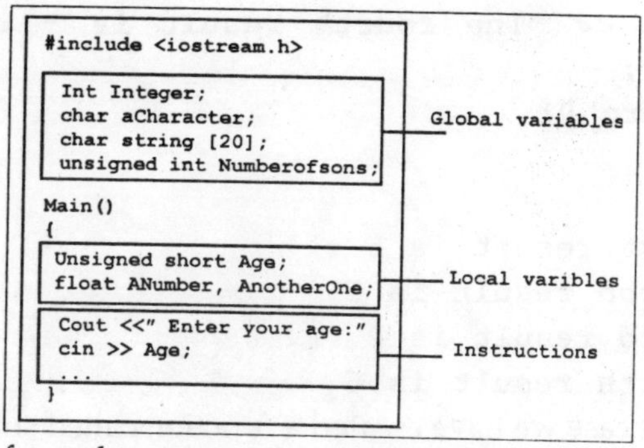


Therefore, the scope of local variables is limited to the same block level in which they are declared. Nevertheless, we also have the possibility to declare global variables; These are visible from any point of the code, inside and outside all functions. In order to declare global variables you simply have to declare the variable outside any function or block; that means, directly in the body of the programme.

*And here is another example about functions*:

```
// function example
#include <iostream>
using namespace std;
int subtraction (int a, int b)
{
    int r;
    r=a-b;
    return (r);
}
int main ()
{
    int x=5, y=3, z;
    z = subtraction (7,2);
    cout << "The first result is " << z <<
    '\n';
    cout << "The second result is " <<
    subtraction (7,2) << '\n';
    cout << "The third result is " << subtraction
    (x,y) << '\n';
    z= 4 + subtraction (x,y);
```

```
    cout << "The fourth result is " << z <<
    '\n';
    return 0;
}
output
The first result is 5
The second result is 5
The third result is 2
The fourth result is 6
```

In this case we have created a function called subtraction. The only thing that this function does is to subtract both passed parameters and to return the result.Nevertheless, if we examine function main we will see that we have made several calls to function subtraction. We have used some different calling methods so that you see other ways or moments when a function can be called.

In order to fully understand these examples you must consider once again that a call to a function could be replaced by the value that the function call itself is going to return. For example, the first case (that you should already know because it is the same pattern that we have used in previous examples):

```
z = subtraction (7,2);
cout << "The first result is " << z;
```

If we replace the function call by the value it returns (*i.e.,* 5), we would have:

```
z = 5;
cout << "The first result is " << z;
```

As well as

```
cout << "The second result is " << subtraction
    (7,2);
```

has the same result as the previous call, but in this case we made the call to subtraction directly as an insertion parameter for cout. Simply consider that the result is the same as if we had written:

```
cout << "The second result is " << 5;
```

since 5 is the value returned by subtraction (7,2).

*In the case of:*

```
cout << "The third result is " << subtraction
```

```
(x,y);
```

The only new thing that we introduced is that the parameters of subtraction are variables instead of constants. That is perfectly valid. In this case the values passed to function subtraction are the values of x and y, that are 5 and 3 respectively, giving 2 as result.The fourth case is more of the same. Simply note that instead of:

```
z = 4 + subtraction (x,y);
```

*we could have written*:

```
z = subtraction (x,y) + 4;
```

with exactly the same result. I have switched places so you can see that the semicolon sign (;) goes at the end of the whole statement. It does not necessarily have to go right after the function call. The explanation might be once again that you imagine that a function can be replaced by its returned value:

```
z = 4 + 2;
z = 2 + 4;
```

Functions with no type. The use of void.

If you remember the syntax of a function declaration:

```
type name ( argument1, argument2 ...)
statement
```

you will see that the declaration begins with a type, that is the type of the function itself (*i.e.*, the type of the datum that will be returned by the function with the return statement). But what if we want to return no value? Imagine that we want to make a function just to show a message on the screen. We do not need it to return any value. In this case we should use the void type specifier for the function. This is a special specifier that indicates absence of type.

```
// void function example
#include <iostream>
using namespace std;
void printmessage ()
{
    cout << "I'm a function!";
}
int main ()
{
```

```
    printmessage ();
    return 0;
}
```

```
output
I'm a function!
```

void can also be used in the function's parameter list to explicitly specify that we want the function to take no actual parameters when it is called. For example, function printmessage could have been declared as:

```
void printmessage (void)
{
    cout << "I'm a function!";
}
```

Although it is optional to specify void in the parameter list. In C++, a parameter list can simply be left blank if we want a function with no parameters. What you must always remember is that the format for calling a function includes specifying its name and enclosing its parameters between parentheses. The non-existence of parameters does not exempt us from the obligation to write the parentheses. For that reason the call to printmessage is:

```
printmessage ();
```

The parentheses clearly indicate that this is a call to a function and not the name of a variable or some other C++ statement.

*The following call would have been incorrect*:

```
printmessage;
```

## FUNCTIONS (II)

Arguments passed by value and by reference. Until now, in all the functions we have seen, the arguments passed to the functions have been passed *by value*. This means that when calling a function with parameters, what we have passed to the function were copies of their values but never the variables themselves. For example, suppose that we called our first function addition using the following code:

```
int x=5, y=3, z;
z = addition ( x , y );
```

What we did in this case was to call to function addition passing the values of x and y, *i.e.* 5 and 3 respectively, but not the variables x and y themselves.

```
Int addition (int a, int b)
               ↑       ↑

z = addition (5,       3);
```

This way, when the function addition is called, the value of its local variables a and b become 5 and 3 respectively, but any modification to either a or b within the function addition will not have any effect in the values of x and y outside it, because variables x and y were not themselves passed to the function, but only copies of their values at the moment the function was called.

But there might be some cases where you need to manipulate from inside a function the value of an external variable. For that purpose we can use arguments passed by reference, as in the function duplicate of the following example:

```
// passing parameters by reference
#include <iostream>
using namespace std;
void duplicate (int& a, int& b, int& c)
{
    a*=2;
    b*=2;
    c*=2;
}
int main ()
{
    int x=1, y=3, z=7;
    duplicate (x, y, z);
    cout << "x=" << x << ", y=" << y << ", z="
    << z;
    return 0;
}
output
x=2, y=6, z=14
```

The first thing that should call your attention is that in the declaration of duplicate the type of each parameter was followed by an ampersand sign (&). This ampersand is what specifies that their corresponding arguments are to be passed *by reference* instead of *by value.*

When a variable is passed by reference we are not passing a copy of its value, but we are somehow passing the variable itself to the function and any modification that we do to the local variables will have an effect in their counterpart variables passed as arguments in the call to the function.

```
Void duplicate (int& a, int& b, int& c)
                    ↕x      ↕       ↕z
     duplicate ( x,      y,      z);
```

To explain it in another way, we associate a, b and c with the arguments passed on the function call (x, y and z) and any change that we do on a within the function will affect the value of x outside it. Any change that we do on b will affect y, and the same with c and z.That is why our program's output, that shows the values stored in x, y and z after the call to duplicate, shows the values of all the three variables of main doubled.

If when declaring the following function:

```
void duplicate (int& a, int& b, int& c)
```

we had declared it this way:

```
void duplicate (int a, int b, int c)
```

*i.e.,* without the ampersand signs (&), we would have not passed the variables by reference, but a copy of their values instead, and therefore, the output on screen of our programme would have been the values of x, y and z without having been modified.

Passing by reference is also an effective way to allow a function to return more than one value. For example, here is a function that returns the previous and next numbers of the first parameter passed.

```
// more than one returning value
#include <iostream>
using namespace std;
void prevnext (int x, int& prev, int& next)
{
    prev = x-1;
    next = x+1;
```

```
}
int main ()
{
    int x=100, y, z;
    prevnext (x, y, z);
    cout << "Previous=" << y << ", Next=" << z;
    return 0;
}
output
Previous=99, Next=101
```

## Default values in parameters

When declaring a function we can specify a default value for each parameter. This value will be used if the corresponding argument is left blank when calling to the function. To do that, we simply have to use the assignment operator and a value for the arguments in the function declaration. If a value for that parameter is not passed when the function is called, the default value is used, but if a value is specified this default value is ignored and the passed value is used instead. For example:

```
// default values in functions
#include <iostream>
using namespace std;
int divide (int a, int b=2)
{
 int r;
 r=a/b;
 return (r);
}
int main ()
{
 cout << divide (12);
 cout << endl;
 cout << divide (20,4);
 return 0;
}
output
```

```
6
5
```

As we can see in the body of the programme there are two calls to function divide. In the first one:

```
divide (12)
```

we have only specified one argument, but the function divide allows up to two. So the function divide has assumed that the second parameter is 2 since that is what we have specified to happen if this parameter was not passed (notice the function declaration, which finishes with int b=2, not just int b). Therefore the result of this function call is 6 (12/2).

*In the second call*:

```
divide (20,4)
```

there are two parameters, so the default value for b (int b=2) is ignored and b takes the value passed as argument, that is 4, making the result returned equal to 5 (20/4).

## Overloaded Functions

In C++ two different functions can have the same name if their parameter types or number are different. That means that you can give the same name to more than one function if they have either a different number of parameters or different types in their parameters.

*For example*:

```
// overloaded function
#include <iostream>
using namespace std;
int operate (int a, int b)
{
    return (a*b);
}
float operate (float a, float b)
{
    return (a/b);
}
int main ()
{
    int x=5,y=2;
```

```
    float n=5.0,m=2.0;
    cout << operate (x,y);
    cout << "\n";
    cout << operate (n,m);
    cout << "\n";
    return 0;
}
output
10 2.5
```

In this case we have defined two functions with the same name, operate, but one of them accepts two parameters of type int and the other one accepts them of type float. The compiler knows which one to call in each case by examining the types passed as arguments when the function is called. If it is called with two ints as its arguments it calls to the function that has two int parameters in its prototype and if it is called with two floats it will call to the one which has two float parameters in its prototype. In the first call to operate the two arguments passed are of type int, therefore, the function with the first prototype is called; This function returns the result of multiplying both parameters. While the second call passes two arguments of type float, so the function with the second prototype is called. This one has a different behaviour: it divides one parameter by the other. So the behaviour of a call to operate depends on the type of the arguments passed because the function has been *overloaded*. Notice that a function cannot be overloaded only by its return type. At least one of its parameters must have a different type.

## Inline Functions

The inline specifier indicates the compiler that inline substitution is preferred to the usual function call mechanism for a specific function. This does not change the behaviour of a function itself, but is used to suggest to the compiler that the code generated by the function body is inserted at each point the function is called, instead of being inserted only once and perform a regular call to it, which generally involves some additional overhead in running time.

*The format for its declaration is:*

```
inline type name ( arguments ... ) {
instructions ... }
```

and the call is just like the call to any other function. You do not have to include the inline keyword when calling the function, only in its declaration. Most compilers already optimize code to generate inline functions when it is more convenient. This specifier only indicates the compiler that inline is preferred for this function.

## Recursivity

Recursivity is the property that functions have to be called by themselves. It is useful for many tasks, like sorting or calculate the factorial of numbers. For example, to obtain the factorial of a number (n!) the mathematical formula would be:

```
n! = n * (n-1) * (n-2) * (n-3) ... * 1
```

more concretely, 5! (factorial of 5) would be:

```
5! = 5 * 4 * 3 * 2 * 1 = 120
```

and a recursive function to calculate this in C++ could be:

```
// factorial calculator
#include <iostream>
using namespace std;
long factorial (long a)
{
    if (a > 1)
    return (a * factorial (a-1));
    else
    return (1);
}
int main ()
{
    long number;
    cout << "Please type a number: ";
    cin >> number;
    cout << number << "! = " << factorial
    (number);
    return 0;
}
```

```
output
Please type a number: 9
9! = 362880
```

Notice how in function factorial we included a call to itself, but only if the argument passed was greater than 1, since otherwise the function would perform an infinite recursive loop in which once it arrived to 0 it would continue multiplying by all the negative numbers (probably provoking a stack overflow error on runtime). This function has a limitation because of the data type we used in its design (long) for more simplicity. The results given will not be valid for values much greater than 10! or 15!, depending on the system you compile it.

## Declaring Functions

Until now, we have defined all of the functions before the first appearance of calls to them in the source code. These calls were generally in function main which we have always left at the end of the source code. If you try to repeat some of the examples of functions described so far, but placing the function main before any of the other functions that were called from within it, you will most likely obtain compiling errors. The reason is that to be able to call a function it must have been declared in some earlier point of the code, like we have done in all our examples.

But there is an alternative way to avoid writing the whole code of a function before it can be used in main or in some other function. This can be achieved by declaring just a prototype of the function before it is used, instead of the entire definition. This declaration is shorter than the entire definition, but significant enough for the compiler to determine its return type and the types of its parameters.

*Its form is:*

```
type name ( argument_type1, argument_type2,
    ...);
```

It is identical to a function definition, except that it does not include the body of the function itself (*i.e.*, the function statements that in normal definitions are enclosed in braces { }) and instead of that we end the prototype declaration with a mandatory semicolon (;). The parameter enumeration does not need to include the identifiers, but only the type specifiers. The inclusion of a name for each parameter as in the function definition is optional in the prototype declaration. For example, we can declare a function called protofunction with two int parameters with any of the following declarations:

```
int protofunction (int first, int second);
int protofunction (int, int);
```

Anyway, including a name for each variable makes the prototype more legible.

```
// declaring functions prototypes
#include <iostream>
using namespace std;
void odd (int a);
void even (int a);
int main ()
{
    int i;
    do {
    cout << "Type a number (0 to exit): ";
  cin >> i;
    odd (i);
    } while (i!=0);
    return 0;
}
void odd (int a)
{
 if ((a%2)!=0) cout << "Number is odd.\n";
 else even (a);
}
void even (int a)
{
    if ((a%2)==0) cout << "Number is even.\n";
    else odd (a);
}
output
Type a number (0 to exit): 9
Number is odd.
```

```
Type a number (0 to exit): 6
Number is even.
Type a number (0 to exit): 1030
Number is even.
Type a number (0 to exit): 0
Number is even.
```

This example is indeed not an example of efficiency. I am sure that at this point you can already make a programme with the same result, but using only half of the code lines that have been used in this example. Anyway this example illustrates how prototyping works. Moreover, in this concrete example the prototyping of at least one of the two functions is necessary in order to compile the code without errors. The first things that we see are the declaration of functions odd and even:

```
void odd (int a);
void even (int a);
```

This allows these functions to be used before they are defined, for example, in main, which now is located where some people find it to be a more logical place for the start of a programme: the beginning of the source code.

Anyway, the reason why this programme needs at least one of the functions to be declared before it is defined is because in odd there is a call to even and in even there is a call to odd. If none of the two functions had been previously declared, a compilation error would happen, since either odd would not not be visible from even (because it has still not been declared), or even would not be visible from odd (for the same reason). Having the prototype of all functions together in the same place within the source code is found practical by some programmers, and this can be easily achieved by declaring all functions prototypes at the beginning of a programme.

## ARRAYS

An array is a series of elements of the same type placed in contiguous memory locations that can be individually referenced by adding an index to a unique identifier. That means that, for example, we can store 5 values of type int in an array without having to declare 5 different variables, each one with a different identifier. Instead of that, using an array we can store 5 different values of the same type, int for example, with a unique identifier. For example, an array to contain 5 integer values of type int called billy could be represented like this:

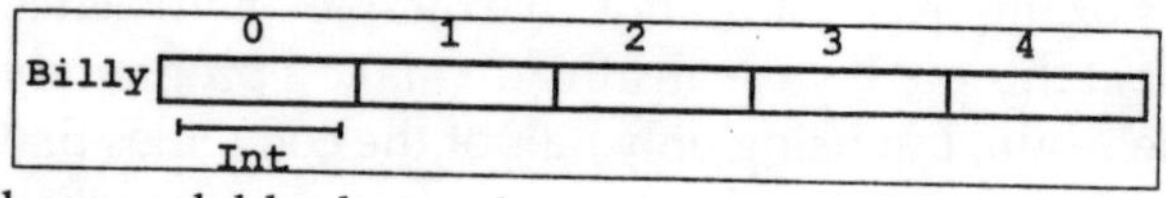


where each blank panel represents an element of the array, that in this case are integer values of type int. These elements are numbered from 0 to 4 since in arrays the first index is always 0, independently of its length.

Like a regular variable, an array must be declared before it is used. A typical declaration for an array in C++ is:

```
type name [elements];
```

where type is a valid type (like int, float...), name is a valid identifier and the elements field (which is always enclosed in square brackets []), specifies how many of these elements the array has to contain.

Therefore, in order to declare an array called billy as the one shown in the above diagram it is as simple as:

```
int billy [5];
```

*Note*: The elements field within brackets [] which represents the number of elements the array is going to hold, must be a constant value, since arrays are blocks of non-dynamic memory whose size must be determined before execution. In order to create arrays with a variable length dynamic memory is needed, which is explained later in these tutorials.

## Initializing Arrays

When declaring a regular array of local scope (within a function, for example), if we do not specify otherwise, its elements will not be initialized to any value by default, so their content will be undetermined until we store some value in them. The elements of global and static arrays, on the other hand, are automatically initialized with their default values, which for all fundamental types this means they are filled with zeros. In both cases, local and global, when we declare an array, we have the possibility to assign initial values to each one of its elements by enclosing the values in braces { }. For example:

```
int billy [5] = { 16, 2, 77, 40, 12071 };
```

*This declaration would have created an array like this:*

| | 0 | 1 | 2 | 3 | 4 |
|---|---|---|---|---|---|
| Billy | 16 | 2 | 77 | 40 | 12071 |

The amount of values between braces { } must not be larger than the number of elements that we declare for the array between square brackets [ ]. For example, in the example of array billy we have declared that it has 5 elements and in the list of initial values within braces { } we have specified 5 values, one for each element.

When an initialization of values is provided for an array, C++ allows the possibility of leaving the square brackets empty [ ]. In this case, the compiler will assume a size for the array that matches the number of values included between braces { }:

```
int billy [] = { 16, 2, 77, 40, 12071 };
```

After this declaration, array billy would be 5 ints long, since we have provided 5 initialization values.

## Accessing the Values of an Array

In any point of a programme in which an array is visible, we can access the value of any of its elements individually as if it was a normal variable, thus being able to both read and modify its value. The format is as simple as:

name[index]

Following the previous examples in which billy had 5 elements and each of those elements was of type int, the name which we can use to refer to each element is the following:

| | Billy[0] | Billy[1] | Billy[2] | Billy[3] | Billy[4] |
|---|---|---|---|---|---|
| Billy | | | | | |

For example, to store the value 75 in the third element of billy, we could write the following statement:

```
billy[2] = 75;
```

and, for example, to pass the value of the third element of billy to a variable called a, we could write:

```
a = billy[2];
```

Therefore, the expression billy[2] is for all purposes like a variable of type int. Notice that the third element of billy is specified billy[2], since the first one is billy[0], the second one is billy[1], and therefore, the third one is billy[2]. By this same reason, its last element is billy[4]. Therefore, if we write billy[5], we would be accessing the sixth element of billy and therefore exceeding the size of the array.

In C++ it is syntactically correct to exceed the valid range of indices for an array. This can create problems, since accessing out-of-range elements do not cause compilation errors but can cause runtime errors. The reason why this is allowed will be seen further ahead when we begin to use pointers. At this point it is important to be able to clearly distinguish between the two uses that brackets [ ] have related to arrays. They perform two different tasks: one is to specify the size of arrays when they are declared; and the second one is to specify indices for concrete array elements. Do not confuse these two possible uses of brackets [ ] with arrays.

```
int billy[5]; // declaration of a new array
billy[2] = 75; // access to an element of the
    array.
```

If you read carefully, you will see that a type specifier always precedes a variable or array declaration, while it never precedes an access.

*Some other valid operations with arrays:*

```
billy[0] = a;
billy[a] = 75;
b = billy [a+2];
billy[billy[a]] = billy[2] + 5;
// arrays example
#include <iostream>
using namespace std;
int billy [] = {16, 2, 77, 40, 12071};
int n, result=0;
int main ()
{
    for ( n=0 ; n<5 ; n++ )
    {
```

```
    result += billy[n];
    }
    cout << result;
    return 0;
}
output
12206
```

## Multidimensional Arrays

Multidimensional arrays can be described as "arrays of arrays". For example, a bidimensional array can be imagined as a bidimensional table made of elements, all of them of a same uniform data type.

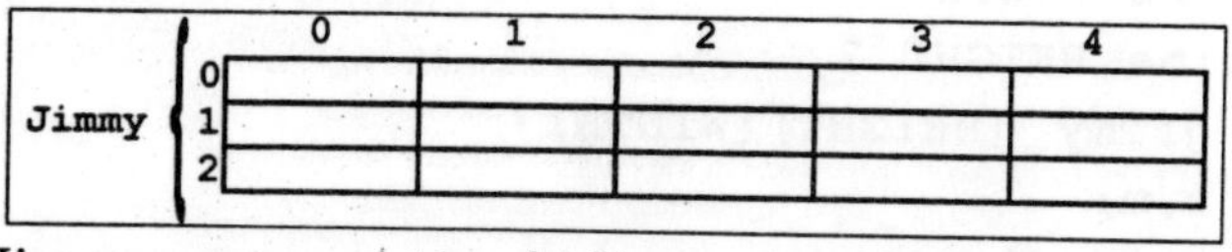


Jimmy represents a bidimensional array of 3 per 5 elements of type int. The way to declare this array in C++ would be:

```
int jimmy [3][5];
```

and, for example, the way to reference the second element vertically and fourth horizontally in an expression would be:

```
jimmy[1][3]
```

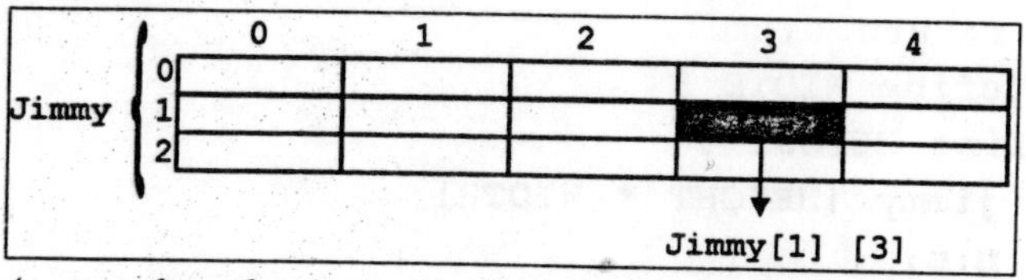


(remember that array indices always begin by zero).

Multidimensional arrays are not limited to two indices (*i.e.*, two dimensions). They can contain as many indices as needed. But be careful! The amount of memory needed for an array rapidly increases with each dimension. For example:

```
char century [100][365][24][60][60];
```

declares an array with a char element for each second in a century, that is more than 3 billion chars. So this declaration would consume more than 3 gigabytes of memory!

Multidimensional arrays are just an abstraction for programmers, since we can obtain the same results with a simple array just by putting a factor between its indices:

```
int jimmy [3][5];   // is equivalent to
int jimmy [15];    // (3 * 5 = 15)
```

With the only difference that with multidimensional arrays the compiler remembers the depth of each imaginary dimension for us.

Take as example these two pieces of code, with both exactly the same result. One uses a bidimensional array and the other one uses a simple array:

multidimensional array pseudo-multidimensional array

```
#define WIDTH 5
#define HEIGHT 3
int jimmy [HEIGHT][WIDTH];
int n,m;
int main ()
{
    for (n=0;n<HEIGHT;n++)
         for (m=0;m<WIDTH;m++)
    {
    jimmy[n][m]=(n+1)*(m+1);
      }
    return 0;
} #define WIDTH 5
#define HEIGHT 3
int jimmy [HEIGHT * WIDTH];
int n,m;
int main ()
{
    for (n=0;n<HEIGHT;n++)
         for (m=0;m<WIDTH;m++)
    {
    jimmy[n*WIDTH+m]=(n+1)*(m+1);
  }
 return 0;
}
```

None of the two source codes above produce any output on the screen, but both assign values to the memory block called jimmy in the following way:

| | | 0 | 1 | 2 | 3 | 4 |
|---|---|---|---|---|---|---|
| Jimmy | 0 | 1 | 2 | 3 | 4 | 5 |
| | 1 | 2 | 4 | 6 | 8 | 10 |
| | 2 | 3 | 6 | 9 | 12 | 15 |

We have used "defined constants" (#define) to simplify possible future modifications of the programme. For example, in case that we decided to enlarge the array to a height of 4 instead of 3 it could be done simply by changing the line:

```
#define HEIGHT 3
```

to:

```
#define HEIGHT 4
```

with no need to make any other modifications to the programme.

## Arrays as Parameters

At some moment we may need to pass an array to a function as a parameter. In C++ it is not possible to pass a complete block of memory by value as a parameter to a function, but we are allowed to pass its address. In practice this has almost the same effect and it is a much faster and more efficient operation. In order to accept arrays as parameters the only thing that we have to do when declaring the function is to specify in its parameters the element type of the array, an identifier and a pair of void brackets []. For example, the following function:

```
void procedure (int arg[])
```

accepts a parameter of type "array of int" called arg. In order to pass to this function an array declared as:

```
int myarray [40];
```

it would be enough to write a call like this:

```
procedure (myarray);
```

Here you have a complete example:

```
// arrays as parameters
#include <iostream>
using namespace std;
```

```
void printarray (int arg[], int length) {
    for (int n=0; n<length; n++)
        cout << arg[n] << " ";
    cout << "\n";
}
int main ()
{
    int firstarray[] = {5, 10, 15};
    int secondarray[] = {2, 4, 6, 8, 10};
    printarray (firstarray,3);
    printarray (secondarray,5);
    return 0;
}
output
5 10 15 2 4 6 8 10
```

As you can see, the first parameter (int arg[]) accepts any array whose elements are of type int, whatever its length. For that reason we have included a second parameter that tells the function the length of each array that we pass to it as its first parameter. This allows the for loop that prints out the array to know the range to iterate in the passed array without going out of range.

In a function declaration it is also possible to include multidimensional arrays. The format for a tridimensional array parameter is:

**base_type[][depth][depth]**

for example, a function with a multidimensional array as argument could be:

**void procedure (int myarray[][3][4])**

Notice that the first brackets [] are left blank while the following ones are not. This is so because the compiler must be able to determine within the function which is the depth of each additional dimension.

Arrays, both simple or multidimensional, passed as function parameters are a quite common source of errors for novice programmers. I recommend the reading of the chapter about Pointers for a better understanding on how arrays operate.

## CHARACTER SEQUENCES

As you may already know, the C++ Standard Library implements a powerful string class, which is very useful to handle and manipulate strings of characters. However, because strings are in fact sequences of characters, we can represent them also as plain arrays of char elements.

*For example, the following array:*

```
char jenny [20];
```

is an array that can store up to 20 elements of type char. It can be represented as:

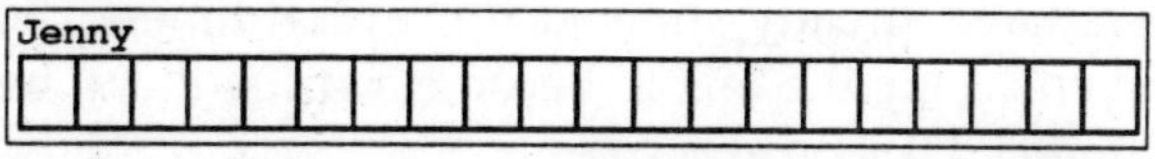


Therefore, in this array, in theory, we can store sequences of characters up to 20 characters long. But we can also store shorter sequences. For example, jenny could store at some point in a programme either the sequence "Hello" or the sequence "Merry christmas", since both are shorter than 20 characters.

Therefore, since the array of characters can store shorter sequences than its total length, a special character is used to signal the end of the valid sequence: the *null character*, whose literal constant can be written as '\0' (backslash, zero). Our array of 20 elements of type char, called jenny, can be represented storing the characters sequences "Hello" and "Merry Christmas" as:

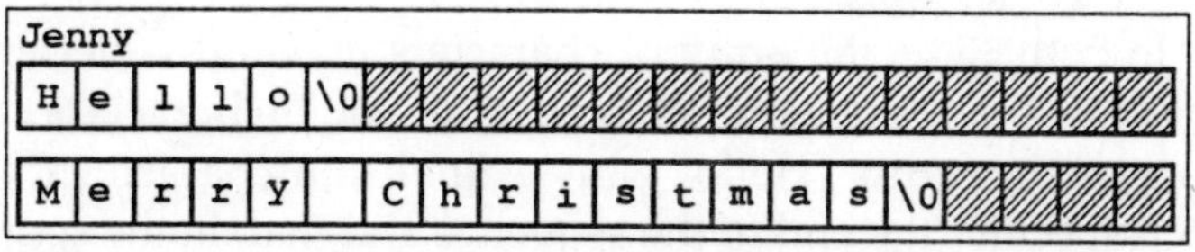


Notice how after the valid content a null character ('\0') has been included in order to indicate the end of the sequence. The panels in gray colour represent char elements with undetermined values.

### Initialization of Null-terminated Character Sequences

Because arrays of characters are ordinary arrays they follow all their same rules. For example, if we want to initialize an array of characters with some predetermined sequence of characters we can do it just like any other array:

```
char myword[] = { 'H', 'e', 'l', 'l', 'o',
'\0' };
```

In this case we would have declared an array of 6 elements of type char initialized with the characters that form the word "Hello" plus a null character '\0' at the end.

But arrays of char elements have an additional method to initialize their values: using string literals.

In the expressions we have used in some examples in previous chapters, constants that represent entire strings of characters have already showed up several times. These are specified enclosing the text to become a string literal between double quotes ("). For example:

```
"the result is: "
```

is a constant string literal that we have probably used already.

Double quoted strings (") are literal constants whose type is in fact a null-terminated array of characters. So string literals enclosed between double quotes always have a null character ('\0') automatically appended at the end.

Therefore we can initialize the array of char elements called myword with a null-terminated sequence of characters by either one of these two methods:

```
char myword [] = { 'H', 'e', 'l', 'l', 'o',
'\0' };
char myword [] = "Hello";
```

In both cases the array of characters myword is declared with a size of 6 elements of type char: the 5 characters that compose the word "Hello" plus a final null character ('\0') which specifies the end of the sequence and that, in the second case, when using double quotes (") it is appended automatically.

Please notice that we are talking about initializing an array of characters in the moment it is being declared, and not about assigning values to them once they have already been declared. In fact because this type of null-terminated arrays of characters are regular arrays we have the same restrictions that we have with any other array, so we are not able to copy blocks of data with an assignment operation. Assuming mystext is a char[] variable, expressions within a source code like:

```
mystext = "Hello";
mystext[] = "Hello";
```

would not be valid, like neither would be:

```
mystext = { 'H', 'e', 'l', 'l', 'o', '\0' };
```

The reason for this may become more comprehensible once you know a bit more about pointers, since then it will be clarified that an array is in fact a constant pointer pointing to a block of memory.

## Using Null-terminated Sequences of Characters

Null-terminated sequences of characters are the natural way of treating strings in C++, so they can be used as such in many procedures. In fact, regular string literals have this type (char[]) and can also be used in most cases.

For example, cin and cout support null-terminated sequences as valid containers for sequences of characters, so they can be used directly to extract strings of characters from cin or to insert them into cout. For example:

```
// null-terminated sequences of characters
#include <iostream>
using namespace std;

int main ()
{
 char question[] = "Please, enter your first
    name: ";
 char greeting[] = "Hello, ";
 char yourname [80];
 cout << question;
 cin >> yourname;
 cout << greeting << yourname << "!";
 return 0;
}
output
Please, enter your first name: John
Hello, John!
```

As you can see, we have declared three arrays of char elements. The first two were initialized with string literal constants, while the third one was left uninitialized. In any case, we have to speficify the size of the array: in the first two (question and greeting) the size was implicitly defined by the length of the literal constant they were initialized to. While for yourname we have explicitly specified that it has a size of 80 chars. Finally, sequences of characters stored in char arrays can easily be converted into string objects just by using the assignment operator:

```
string mystring;
char myntcs[]="some text";
mystring = myntcs;
```

## POINTERS

We have already seen how variables are seen as memory cells that can be accessed using their identifiers. This way we did not have to care about the physical location of our data within memory, we simply used its identifier whenever we wanted to refer to our variable.

The memory of your computer can be imagined as a succession of memory cells, each one of the minimal size that computers manage (one byte). These single-byte memory cells are numbered in a consecutive way, so as, within any block of memory, every cell has the same number as the previous one plus one. This way, each cell can be easily located in the memory because it has a unique address and all the memory cells follow a successive pattern. For example, if we are looking for cell 1776 we know that it is going to be right between cells 1775 and 1777, exactly one thousand cells after 776 and exactly one thousand cells before cell 2776.

### Reference Operator (&)

As soon as we declare a variable, the amount of memory needed is assigned for it at a specific location in memory (its memory address). We generally do not actively decide the exact location of the variable within the panel of cells that we have imagined the memory to be - Fortunately, that is a task automatically performed by the operating system during runtime. However, in some cases we may be interested in knowing the address where our variable is being stored during runtime in order to operate with relative positions to it.

The address that locates a variable within memory is what we call a *reference* to that variable. This reference to a variable can be obtained by preceding the identifier of a variable with an ampersand sign (&), known as reference operator, and which can be literally translated as "address of". For example:

```
ted = &andy;
```

This would assign to ted the address of variable andy, since when preceding the name of the variable andy with the reference operator (&) we are no longer talking about the content of the variable itself, but about its reference (*i.e.*, its address in memory). For now on we are going to assume that andy is placed during runtime in the memory address 1776. This number (1776) is just and arbitrary assumption we are inventing right now in order to help clarify some concepts in this tutorial, but in reality, we cannot know before runtime the real value the address of a variable will have in memory.

*Consider the following code fragment*:

```
andy = 25;
fred = andy;
ted = &andy;
```

The values contained in each variable after the execution of this, are shown in the following diagram:

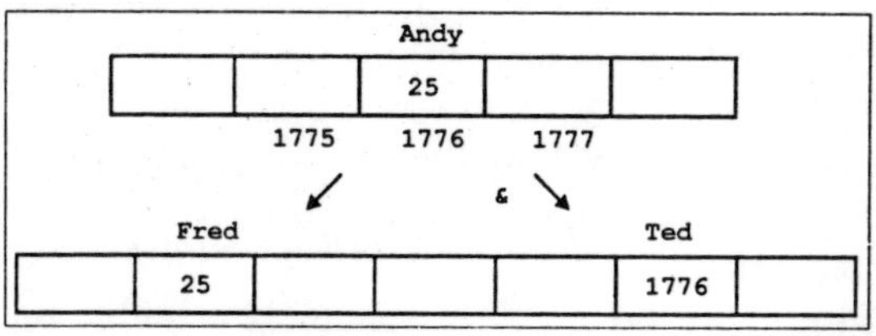


First, we have assigned the value 25 to andy (a variable whose address in memory we have assumed to be 1776). The second statement copied to fred the content of variable andy (which is 25). This is a standard assignment operation, as we have done so many times before. Finally, the third statement copies to ted not the value contained in andy but a reference to it (*i.e.*, its address, which we have assumed to be 1776).The reason is that in this third assignment operation we have preceded the identifier andy with the reference operator (&), so we were no longer referring to the value of andy but to its reference (its address in memory).

The variable that stores the reference to another variable (like ted in the previous example) is what we call a *pointer*. Pointers are a very powerful feature of the C++ language that has many uses in advanced programming. Farther ahead, we will see how this type of variable is used and declared.

### Pointer Arithmetics

To conduct arithmetical operations on pointers is a little different than to conduct them on regular integer data types. To begin with, only addition and subtraction operations are allowed to be conducted with them, the others make no sense in the world of pointers.

But both addition and subtraction have a different behaviour with pointers according to the size of the data type to which they point. When we saw the different fundamental data types, we saw that some occupy more or less space than others in the memory.

For example, let's assume that in a given compiler for a specific machine, char takes 1 byte, short takes 2 bytes and long takes 4.

Suppose that we define three pointers in this compiler:

```
char *mychar;
short *myshort;
long *mylong;
```

and that we know that they point to memory locations 1000, 2000 and 3000 respectively.

*So if we write:*

```
mychar++;
myshort++;
mylong++;
```

mychar, as you may expect, would contain the value 1001. But not so obviously, myshort would contain the value 2002, and mylong would contain 3004, even though they have each been increased only once. The reason is that when adding one to a pointer we are making it to point to the following element of the same type with which it has been defined, and therefore the size in bytes of the type pointed is added to the pointer.

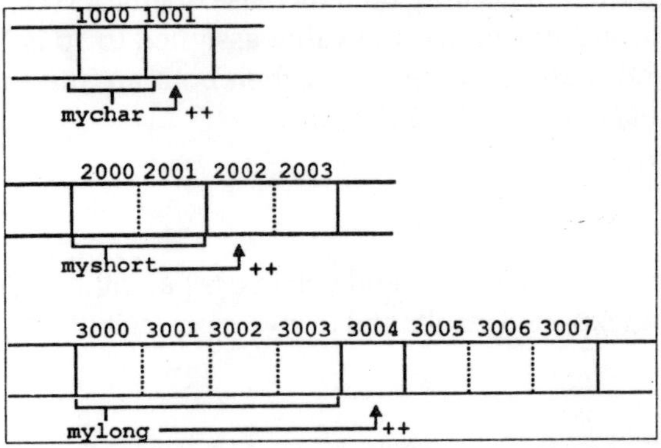


This is applicable both when adding and subtracting any number to a pointer. It would happen exactly the same if we write:

```
mychar = mychar + 1;
myshort = myshort + 1;
mylong = mylong + 1;
```

Both the increase (++) and decrease (—) operators have greater operator precedence than the dereference operator (*), but both have a special behaviour when used as suffix (the expression is evaluated with the value it had before being increased). Therefore, the following expression may lead to confusion:

```
*p++
```

Because ++ has greater precedence than *, this expression is equivalent to *(p++). Therefore, what it does is to increase the value of p (so it now points to the next element), but because ++ is used as postfix the whole expression is evaluated as the value pointed by the original reference (the address the pointer pointed to before being increased).

Notice the difference with:

```
(*p)++
```

Here, the expression would have been evaluated as the value pointed by p increased by one. The value of p (the pointer itself) would not be modified (what is being modified is what it is being pointed to by this pointer).

*If we write:*

```
*p++ = *q++;
```

Because ++ has a higher precedence than *, both p and q are increased, but because both increase operators (++) are used as postfix and not prefix, the value assigned to *p is *q before both p and q are increased. And then both are increased.

*It would be roughly equivalent to:*

```
*p = *q;
++p;
++q;
```

Like always, I recommend you to use parentheses () in order to avoid unexpected results and to give more legibility to the code.

# Bibliography


Aberth Oliver: *Introduction to Precise Numerical Methods Using C++*, London: Academic Press, 2005.

Alexandrescu Andrei: *Modern C++ Design: Generic Programming and Design Patterns Applied*, New York: Addison-Wesley Press, 2003.

Blanchette Jasmin: *C++ GUI Programming with Qt 4*, London: Prentice-Hall, 2006.

Bulka Dov: *Efficient C++: Performance Programming Techniques*, New York: Addison-Wesley Press, 2003.

Carrano M.: *Data Abstraction and Problem Solving in C++: Walls and Mirrors*, New York: Addison-Wesley Press, 2003.

Ford William H.: *Data Structures with C++ Using STL*, London: Prentice Hall, 2003.

Goodrich T.: *Roberto Tamassia, and David Mount, Data Structures and Algorithms in C++*, New York: John Wiley & Sons Publication, 2001.

Henning Michi: *Advanced CORBA Programming with C++*, New York: Application Development Advisor Company, 2001.

Kruse Robert: *Data Structures and Program Design in C++*, London: Prentice-Hall, 2002.

Lakos John, *Large-Scale C++ Software Design*, New York: Microsoft Press, 2003.

Lippman Stanley B.: *Inside the C++ Object Model*, London: Manning Publications, 2003.

Lischner Ray: *STL Pocket Reference*, New York: O'Reilly Media, 2003.

Mesick: *Maximum MIDI: Music Applications in C++*, London: Manning Publications, 2004.

Meyers Scott: *Effective C++: 55 Specific Ways to Improve Your Programs and Designs*, New York: Addison-Wesley Press, 2001.

Peters T.: *Pattern Recognition with Neural Networks in C++*, London: CRC Press, 2006.

Plauger P. J.: *The C++ Standard Template Library : A Definitive Approach to C++ Programming Using STL*, London: Prentice-Hall, 2003.

Sedgewick Robert: *Algorithms in C++, Parts 1-4: Fundamentals, Data Structures, Sorting, Searching*, London: Cambridge University Press, 2001.

Sedgewick Robert: *Algorithms in C++, Part 5: Graph Algorithms*, New York: Beedle & Associates, 2001.

Stroustrup Bjarne: *The Design and Evolution of C++*, London: Cambridge University, 2003.

Sutter Herb: *C++ Coding Standards: Rules, Guidelines, and Best Practices*, New York: John Wiley & Sons Publication, 2001.

Stephen: *C++ Gotchas: Avoiding Common Problems in Coding and Design*: New York: Digital Systems Research Center Research Report, 2001.

Vandevoorde D.: *C++ Templates - The Complete Guide*, New York: O'Reilly Media, 2003.

Weiss Allen: *Data Structures and Problem Solving Using C++*, London: Manning Publications, 2003.

# Index